Hidden Treasures

Sneaking Love and Health into Every Bite

Survival strategies for parents with picky eaters.

GINA D. DIAMOND, M.ED.

BALBOA.
PRESS

A DIVISION OF HAY HOUSE

Balboa Press books may be ordered through booksellers or by contacting:

Balboa Press
A Division of Hay House
1663 Liberty Drive
Bloomington, IN 47403
www.balboapress.com
1 (877) 407-4847

Because of the dynamic nature of the Internet, any web addresses or links contained in this book may have changed since publication and may no longer be valid. The views expressed in this work are solely those of the author and do not necessarily reflect the views of the publisher, and the publisher hereby disclaims any responsibility for them.

The author of this book does not dispense medical advice or prescribe the use of any technique as a form of treatment for physical, emotional, or medical problems without the advice of a physician, either directly or indirectly. The intent of the author is only to offer information of a general nature to help you in your quest for emotional and spiritual well-being. In the event you use any of the information in this book for yourself, which is your constitutional right, the author and the publisher assume no responsibility for your actions.

Any people depicted in stock imagery provided by Thinkstock are models,
and such images are being used for illustrative purposes only.
Certain stock imagery © Thinkstock.

Print information available on the last page.

ISBN: 978-1-5043-7388-3 (sc)
ISBN: 978-1-5043-7389-0 (e)

Balboa Press rev. date: 07/06/2018

For Lily, my daughter
And all children who deserve health-promoting food and a thriving body

Contents

Foreword

All children deserve nutritious food and much love. So do their parents. Well, Gina Diamond offers both in her book, plus smart ways to enrich the daily meals in most creative ways. Surprising and enticing, the least expected combinations such as cauliflower in pastry dough or purslane in fruit juices, sprung from her hands and pots, to the delight of mothers and cooks alike. Recognizing the merits of organic farmers and health-concerned nutritionists, the author prepares, informs and teaches deliciously the conscientious consumer or parent. So pertinent and valid are her calls to action: "It is time to open up to some truths about what it will take to reach our highest potential." For indeed, without proper nourishment, clean, fresh water, air and nature, our bodies and minds cannot attain the peak performance they should. The superb harmony they could. Many diseases and much suffering today are triggered by nutrients' insufficiency, and most of our commercially grown food is at fault. To feed but also to educate our taste and cravings - are Gina's compulsions. She brilliantly succeeds in this book. Concerned about industrially farmed animals as well as over-consumption of polluted meat, the author excluded this from her original recipes, for good reasons, but one can add it as fish or poultry to the final meal. She emphasizes a plant-based diet, raw cooking, and embraces *Moringa oleifera* - my favorite tree, vegetable, healer and "mother's best friend", as this miraculous plant is affectionately known in some parts of the world. If you are a busy professional or stay-home parent, there is something of value in this book for you to prepare and enjoy. And, as the book advises, stop counting calories and focus on listening to your own body's needs, cherish the wholesome food, and notice your health improving. I advocated for these for long time therefore found pleasure in Gina's wisdom. Other "diamonds", err, pearls from the book remind us to pay the due attention to the environment, aka containers, in which the food is cooked, as many are not safe and can leach toxic chemicals. Not a small detail! Last, but not least, Gina Diamond sneaks love and health in her recipes, but not genetically modified organisms (GMOs), and I think that is perfect. Prevalent and pervasive, unlabeled and hidden in many processed foods, the GMOs were never proven safe for consumption in humans on the long run.

Just a few precious gems from Diamond's "Hidden treasures"…

- Dr Monica Marcu, PharmD, PhD

Acknowledgments

My deepest gratitude goes to my daughter. For her sake, I thought of putting hidden treasures in food she likes. She assisted as my taster to help refine the recipes in this book. Thanks to my parents who proofread several versions of my proposal and for encouraging me to forge my own path on a long and winding road. Thank you to my brother and his friends at Scorpion Design for building me my first website. Thank you to Richard for putting up with my strong desire to feed my family well even though it wasn't your thing.

I appreciate my mentors Amy McKenzie and Tanja Diamond, who walked me past bouts of grief, self-doubt, and writer's block. I am so grateful for my best friend, Eva Live. Her courage to raise human consciousness inspires me and her journey encourages me to reach my potential. I am equally grateful for all my spirit guides who support me in numerous ways.

Thank you also goes out to Clarissa Fetrow who proofread an original version of this book, which is now the foundation of the Making Conscious Eating Choices section. I am also grateful to Danielle Steele who read a draft and made corrections.

Thank you to all my friends and family who sent money for food and equipment, which gave me the time to experiment in the kitchen. I also appreciate the group of people who tried out my recipes and gave me feedback. The person who went above and beyond in this area is Mary Pat Champeau. Thank you for picking up the slack when others weren't able to keep their commitments. And a huge shout out to the Institute for Humane Education, which offered the best educational experience of my life, believed in my potential, and inspired me to end my love affair with cheese.

Several companies donated food to be used to test out my ideas, and a couple people shared their favorite recipes. I was loyal to these companies and nutritional experts and used their products before I began writing my book. They are Artisana, Navitas, Nutiva, Vega, Brendan Brazier, and The Juice Lady.

Thank you to all the true pioneers in nutrition who have made it their life's work to make sure that people have the information they need to make conscious choices. Most importantly, thank you to all the sustainable farmers who are committed to growing the best food possible. In a world where large corporations have support from our government to manipulate the integrity of food and spray artificial chemicals on crops, all the while getting tax cuts, it is nothing short of a miracle that these farmers continue to persevere. I appreciate that they love the land and real food, and are truly dedicated to making sure that we have access to the best, most nutrient-dense produce possible. My body, mind, and spirit say thank you.

Introduction

Perhaps you picked up this book because you spend time with children—either as a parent, teacher, or guardian—and want to make sure that the little ones who surround you are as healthy as possible. Perhaps you picked it up because you wish to adjust your eating habits and model to your loved ones the importance of eating well. Perhaps you are aware of the many benefits of eating mostly plants, and yet find it challenging to get your kids to eat more nutrient-rich foods. Whatever the reason, I am here to tell you that the starting point is to begin creating an environment that gently encourages good eating habits without judgment or conflict.

This book is based on my experience as a mother—trying to feed my family as many plant-based, whole foods as possible while offering mealtimes that are full of connection and joy rather than resistance and disagreements. I have a thirteen-year-old daughter who, left to her own devices, would choose to snack on soft drinks, candy, and French fries. This book is for her and for all of you who seek a creative way to add healthful surprises to your family's meal plan in a joyful way.

I have chosen to focus on what goes into the meals you will create versus on their presentation. Plus, I like the idea of using less paper and offering a less expensive book. As a result, I have elected not to include pictures of the finished product. However, I would love to receive pictures showcasing the meals you create from my recipes in order to post them on my blog and in our Facebook community. Please email them to me at gina@consciouslivingstrategist.com, with or without your family in the picture.

Our Story

Most of you have read the statistics and some of you are living them. Diseases such as obesity, diabetes, heart disease, and cancer have been on the rise for many years. You or a member of your family may be experiencing ill health now. Or you may be one of the lucky ones who is ahead of the game and putting your time and energy into preventing maladies from occurring in the future. Although the realities of today's world can be heartbreaking, the time has come when we can no longer keep our head in the sand. It is time to open up to some truths about what it will take to reach our highest potential. Because you picked up this book, you can rest assured that somewhere within you, no matter how hidden, a desire is awakening to increase the vitality and wellbeing of your own physical being or that of another. Well done! In this case, it is important to grow your knowledge of the relationship between food and health. This book and the following recipes will help you take an important step on the wellness journey. It is exciting to keep deepening our understanding of nutrition and its connection to health while increasing our desire for real whole food.

What's a mother to do?

For the first four years of my daughter's life, she was happy to eat a variety of colorful vegetables and other growing foods. When she began to be exposed to a broader diversity of people and situations, her eating habits began to change. She no longer wanted to eat the variety of nutrient-dense foods, as the allure of highly processed, sugar-laden items was more enticing and addictive. She slowly but steadily began rejecting many of the wonderful foods she had eaten for years and yearned to eat what others packed in their lunches. This scenario is not exclusive to me. Many of you have shared a similar story, and I feel for you because I have obviously been there. Since I don't believe in forcing children, or anyone, to eat a certain quantity or type of food, I got creative and began hiding food in the things that they would eat: purslane in fruit smoothies, radish tops in fruit leathers, spinach in pizza crusts, beet juice in muffins, cauliflower in bread dough, squash in cookies, and so forth. The plant-based items, many of which are raw vegetables, have become what I now call hidden treasures—nutrient-rich ingredients that my family initially didn't know they were consuming, hidden in foods they like! My daughter and her friends now beg me to make the delicious recipes you will find on the following pages. They love these recipes, and I believe the children and kids-at-heart in your life will love them, too.

Everyone can do with a few more growing foods, don't you agree?

Nutritional Understanding

Along my journey to search for answers, I became increasingly aware that out of all the lifestyle choices available, the foods we consume have a huge impact on our well-being. In fact, in the book *The Pleasure Trap*, authors Doug Lisle, Ph.D. and Alan Goldhamer, D.C., write that food is the number one lifestyle choice that dictates whether we are healthy and free of disease. So where has my understanding of nutrition come from? With so many nutritional experts, many of whom disagree with each other, it can be quite challenging to navigate all the literature and come out with a clear notion of which foods promote health and which promote disease.

I can't say with absolute certainty that there is one eating path that creates and maintains health for everyone or that one expert holds the single truth. However, I can say that after years of research there are some fundamental pieces of knowledge that are shared by many of the top nutritional experts. At the same time I remain open, have a curious mind, and am willing to explore as new insights become available.

At a bare minimum, we need to know that a large number of people are nutritionally deficient in many areas. According to the US Department of Agriculture, 74 percent of us have deficiencies as a result of not eating enough fiber, essential fatty acids, minerals, and vitamins. So what are we eating? Bill Sears, M.D. says many of us have adopted the standard American diet, or SAD, which is:

- high in animal fats
- high in saturated and hydrogenated (trans) fats
- low in fiber
- high in processed foods
- low in complex carbohydrates
- low in plant-based foods

The consequences of the standard American diet are clearly having a huge negative effect on the health of North Americans. Extremely high instances of obesity, cardiovascular disease, diabetes, high cholesterol, and other health problems are largely due to the food that we eat, claims the Physicians Committee for Responsible Medicine.

T. Colin Campbell who has a Ph.D. in Nutritional Biochemistry wrote a book called *The China Study*, which the *New York Times* dubbed "the most comprehensive book on nutrition to date." This book details the influence of food processors on the traditional USDA food pyramid, which schools, hospitals, health professionals, and countless individuals have used for decades as a primary source for nutritional guidance. Campbell writes in depth about his experience sitting on numerous boards where he regularly witnessed advisors making dietary recommendations, even though they were simultaneously being bankrolled by subsidiaries of the meat and dairy industries. The conflicts of interest were obvious. For this reason, some physicians and nutritionists have begun to move away from the conventional food pyramid in an effort to find a better way. Many leaders in the health field have responded by creating their own food recommendations. The common thread that binds many of these recommendations is a diet based primarily on whole plant-based foods, with a heavy emphasis on vegetables.

Book Contents

Aside from offering recipes to prepare delicious drinks, snacks, sides, meals, and desserts based on the hidden treasures concept and strategies to get your picky eater to eat well, you now have a brief overview of groundbreaking research that paves a path for the reason nutrition matters. This will be the foundation from which you can compare your current eating habits and begin making new conscious choices that increase your health, one step at a time.

You will notice that the recipes in this book do not contain meat. That is intentional, and I am certainly not advocating a meat-free diet for everyone, so feel free to add animal products to these recipes if you feel your body is in need. Stick to eating animal products that were raised on small farms, ate a natural diet, and roamed freely as well as wild fish. Four ounces per person per meal is a good rule of thumb for meat consumption (I put fish and poultry in this category).

Road Markers

To transition the family into a more health-supporting way of eating, many recipes include road markers offering food suggestions and preparation tips that deepen the hidden treasures experience. Look for the heading, Nutritional Nugget(s), for information that relates to the nutritional value of food and Tasty Gem(s) for food-buying tips, serving suggestions, or adaptations. You may ignore the road markers for a simpler approach. You could start by focusing on one section at a time, implementing all of the suggestions before moving on. Or read from front to back, taking it all in! Set yourself up for success by picking the path that feels best for you.

Recipes

The majority of my recipes are for time conscious, busy parents. However, some include instructions that offer additional steps to cook from scratch and/or prepare raw food. Trying out these additional steps could come later when you feel confident and ready to take on a new challenge. For this reason, the recipes have a level of flexibility new to cookbooks. The ingredients are often interchangeable, meaning you can substitute spinach for zucchini in a specific recipe. The main thing to be aware of is how well the main or "likeable" ingredients are camouflaging the hidden treasure. Stick to the recipes as they are for now. Once you get a hang of this system, feel free to experiment. Variations come in handy when you find yourself without a certain ingredient during the cooking process, or if there is a better local alternative. Enjoy, and thanks for being part of the solution!

No Calorie Counting - You will probably notice that I did not include calorie counts at the end of my recipes. Like everything else, people have strong opinions about counting calories. I am opposed to this and yet I realize there is probably a place for counting calories.

I find that people can become too focused on this activity and miss the main point of eating, which is to enjoy the experience while fueling their body. It is important to note that just because something doesn't have a lot of calories doesn't mean that it is nutritious or even meant for human consumption. Low-calorie and low-fat can often mean artificial (a.k.a not good for you) or striped of nutrition and replaced with taste tantalizers that your body doesn't need. Besides being highly time consuming, counting calories can be worrisome (not good for your health) and misleading. Meals often have more calories than stated, especially if made from processed foods. Plus, it takes more calories to digest certain foods, so going by the label alone is not always painting the whole picture. Also, some people absorb more than others, so calorie intakes can differ from person to person even if the same food is consumed. Besides, quality is considerably more important than quantity. Calories are a good thing providing that you don't stuff yourself and eat nutrient-dense whole foods at least 80% of the time. Most importantly, I advocate eating intuitively. Listen to what your body needs and stop eating before you get full.

A Treasure Trove of Tips

Additional ideas to get family members to eat well

Even though I love the hidden treasure recipe method, I do not rely on it as the only way to get healthful food into my family. It is but one tool in a box of many. It is for that reason that this section is dedicated to offering additional ways to encourage good eating habits without cajoling, bribing, punishing, rewarding, or praising. Top of the list is "**model the message**"! Do you think your child will eat well if you don't? Parents are the number one influence in a child's life until around the age of 11 when peers begin to have a stronger pull. We have 11 years folks to plant some seeds. Even if your child eats poorly during the teen years, research shows that most will come back to the values of the family during the later years, so get planting. If the adults in your children's lives (including teachers and caregivers) eat and serve health-sustaining food, you have a much better chance of engaging your kids in this healthful activity.

When modeling the healthful food message **make a big deal** about how great good food tastes and how great you feel after making positive choices, but be sure to be authentic. Do the same when you eat food that makes your body hurt or reduces your energy level. When I eat out with my family and consume something that is heavier than I am used to, I always feel sluggish and I let my daughter know it.

Get your family involved in meals and help to make the rituals around eating special. Perhaps your child will enjoy creating a fancy table setting on an ordinary day or cooking for the family. My daughter wrote a cookbook alongside me, and although not all her recipes are healthful, I am grateful she is learning about food.

Make mealtime fun by following themes such as "try something new night" or "eat a rainbow for a snack." Preparing a salad bar with all sorts of different color vegetables can often encourage creativity and consumption. Try suggesting that your little ones make a face out of their vegetables and see how creative they can get. You can even play the guessing game where an adult guesses the order in which a child will eat her/his healthful food. See how close you can get! Or you can guess how many of a particular type of food your child will eat.

Think outside the box. Break mindsets by serving vegetables at breakfast, either by offering green smoothies or having a plate of cut up produce on the table. Your kids just may start asking for carrots when they first wake up.

Hang alternative food charts on the refrigerator, such as the one created by the Physicians for Responsible Medicine site. The food chart encourages kids and kids-at-heart to eat more organic unprocessed vegetables, whole sprouted grains, and raw fruits. Seeing charts everyday will offset some of the advertisements your kids are exposed to in school, at the grocery store, and on the television and billboards that promote fast-food type of eating.

Cut foods into small pieces, as kids are more willing to try something new when they do not have to fit a huge piece of something unusual in their mouth. This also works for adults.

Suggest that your child **organize a food-trying party**, and invite a bunch of your childrens' friends over. Kids are more willing to try something new if their friends will. And remember that this is a journey, so relax and go with the flow if your child makes a face or refuses to try something new. Keep offering, and remember that some kids need to try the same thing over and over before their tastes buds become acclimated to a new taste or texture.

Try handing out vegetables liberally when your family is enjoying **special time**, such as playing a board game or ending a family meeting. This will offset the message that special time must be accompanied by junk food.

Bring healthful snacks on **family outings** so that you are not bombarded with hungry kids and at the whim of fast-food snack options. I find that riding the public bus is an exceptionally great time to have my offerings accepted. There is something about a long bus ride home from a long day of activities that opens the door for adventurous food trying.

Begin to **let go of foods** that do not serve the human body one item at a time as you introduce new healthful foods to your family. For example, consider making raw bars to consume on hiking trips instead of protein bars that may contain artificial ingredients and have been heat processed. Homemade options are even better than organic varieties you find at health food stores.

Make eating wholesome foods easy by preparing snacks before you want to eat them. That way when your busy family is hungry, a wholesome snack is accessible on the fly and you will not be as tempted to grab processed convenience foods. You can prepare several recipes, including those in this book before the week begins or you can simply wash and cut veggies and store them in an airtight container for when hunger strikes.

As a last resort, **supplement with vitamins**, especially while your family members are in the process of making new and healthful food habits. Look for supplements that are organic, come from whole food sources, and are preferably less processed (raw). Be sure to do some research to find a company you trust or use the online Better World Shopping Guide to assist you.

Nutritional Nugget: Consume the most nutrient dense plant in its best form, and you might find that your kid's desire to crave other healthy food options is ignited.

I am so taken with this plant and what it can do to help the body self-correct. The National Institutes of Health claim that it "reverses malnutrition in children in 21 days or less." As such I put my name behind the best variety of this plant known as *Moringa Oleifera*. You can even purchase it for your kids in chocolate or vanilla flavor for those really picky eaters. I give it to my kid and take it daily myself. To see what this **MIRACLE TREE** can do for you go to https://bit.ly/2lrnoHL To purchase go to http://www.ginadiamond.myzija.com/ and select the Enroll button, top right, and search for moringa options (contact me at gina@consciouslivingstrategist.com if you want wholesale pricing or suggestions on what to buy).

Making Conscious Eating Choices

Creating health within the family structure is supported by the creation of a space that supports positive choices. Creating such a space is multifaceted because it means obtaining personal health within a holistic framework. Achieving holistic health is very much about the type of food we put in our bodies. It is also about all the other daily choices that support the food life cycle, where and how our food is grown, all aspects of meal preparation and storage, and where leftovers go after we are done eating. In this case, leftovers not only include the unconsumed food, but any packaging the food was in when purchased. The following sections will give you a taste of the options that exist within these daily choices to maximize your health and the wellbeing of planet Earth.

Raising your level of awareness is the first step in beginning to make positive and healthier choices. One way to do that is by becoming familiar with food production and what exactly you are currently eating. The majority of food that you see in the supermarket is grown with the help of toxic chemicals. This is a fairly new way of farming. The use of synthetic pesticides, for example, began in the 1930s, and reliance on this growing method has only increased. This type of farming is referred to as conventional. However, there are farmers all across the country who returned to the old ways of farming because they understand that the health of plants, soil, and waterways directly impacts the health of people. Some of these farmers are choosing to apply for organic certification. While there has been some criticism over the quality of what the organic label means and how well the certification is regulated, generally speaking, food grown organically is not supposed to involve synthetic pesticides or artificial fertilizers, irradiation (a process used to kill bacteria by exposing meat, grains, and other food to high levels of radiation), antibiotics, hormones, sewer sludge, or genetically modified organisms. Many consumers and farmers alike who believe that the organic standards have been weakened are making different choices. Some are supporting and being certified by nonprofit organizations such as biodynamic farming instead of by the United States government. Some farmers have rejected certification altogether and form buddy verification systems whereby farmers collaborate to move toward and maintain green practices. Michael Pollan, author of *In Defense of Food: An Eater's Manifesto*, explains an approach to purchasing food called "Shake the hand that feeds you." This is a great motto to live by and can certainly help you become more aware of the conditions under which your food is grown. Of course, this entails actually meeting farmers who grow your food. This can be done by visiting farms and going to your local farmers' market. In most cases food purchased at these locations will be cheaper and fresher than what you can find at the grocery store. It is accurate that organic food often costs more, but if it is the real deal, it is worth it.

Tasty Gem: Many large farms that use unsustainable practices are getting tax incentives or subsidies from the US government. This means you are actually paying an artificially low price when you purchase food from these conventional farms.

While it is true that the price tag of some wholesome food options is higher, this is only part of the story. There are many avenues to incorporating whole organic foods into one's dietary routine while being sensitive to varying budgets. Community Supported Agriculture (CSA) programs offered by individual farms allow people to purchase a share of harvest in advance at a lower price. Many CSAs have annual, quarterly, monthly, or weekly buy-in membership options and provide deliveries or pickups. Google Local Harvest to find a farm in your area.

Growing your own food is considerably cheaper, especially if you plant seeds instead of buying plant starts. If you do not have a back yard, try growing things inside, at your local community garden, or in pots on a balcony or rooftop. Purchasing food in bulk (large quantities) also saves money. And if all else fails, you can start by purchasing just those organically grown items that are routinely on the "dirty dozen" list that is put out by The Environmental Working Group. While the list changes, strawberries, grapes and spinach are routinely included.

We have yet to see all the options available for use in growing and producing. There will continue to be innovation and new technologies to hit farmers as people strive to find the next niche to fulfill consumer trends that weigh heavily in the health and sustainability arenas or make a larger profit. For better or worse, technology keeps advancing. Hydroponics, growing food without soil, is picking up speed, as is genetic modification (genetically altering plants and animals with the goal of achieving a trait that is not normally held by an organism). Some countries require that food containing genetically modified organisms (GMOs) be labeled. The United States currently does not. Common GMO crops include soybeans, corn, cotton, canola, squash and their derivatives (tofu, corn syrup, and cottonseed oil and others).

To raise your level of awareness around food sourcing, another action you can take is to become street-wise when it comes to labels. Know what they mean and what legal backing they have. Some terms such as natural or free-range are not clearly defined or consistently regulated and are backed only by voluntary standards that manufacturers can choose to follow. Certification processes exist that seek to pay workers an equitable wage, regulate work hours, provide a safe work environment, offer financial and technical support, and promote environmental sustainability. One such process is called Fair Trade. However, the response to Fair Trade has been mixed, so your best bet is to know where your food comes from and whether or not you want your dollars to support such endeavors.

In addition to knowing how your produce is grown, it is also important to raise your awareness in terms of how far your food travels from farm to plate. The average meal travels 1,500 miles. We live in a global society when it comes to goods and services and food is no different. Because it takes a lot of energy to ship food long distances and because fresh food loses its nutrient content overtime, the concept of buying local and seasonal has taken off. Buying local can mean different things to different people. Some choose to only eat foods that were grown within a 100-mile radius from where they live. Some choose to purchase foods that were grown within their region. I support the local food movement (food that is grown, processed, and distributed in a particular place in an effort to promote self-reliant food economies where producers and consumers build a relationship). Still, you will notice that my recipes call for food from all across the world. I put a higher priority on truly sustainably grown and nutrient dense food, but I always purchase organic and local whenever I can. I have also begun to grow my own food and dehydrate it for consumption during the winter months. This is not only a conscious choice but it is a health-promoting option as well. I want my food to maintain its Nutritional Nuggets and I encourage you to do the same, one step at a time. For more information about local economies, including farmers' markets, visit North America Balle online.

Sustainable, fairly traded, and local foods are great but there are other factors to consider when purchasing food. Our food system has changed dramatically over the past 50 years. In the United States most of our food is processed and many countries are following suit. In part this is to accommodate busy lifestyles but it is also due to the fact that companies are making billions of dollars as a result of millions of people purchasing prepackaged processed foods. In contrast, whole foods, which are unprocessed, unrefined, and closely resemble the produce at harvest time are real food because they haven't been altered and have most of their nutrients intact. While many of my recipes contain a myriad of whole foods, many have undergone some processing such as cooking, dehydration, and blending. This is a whole lot better than purchasing fast food, frozen dinners, pasteurized (the process of using heat and fast cooling to destroy pathogens in food), and prepackaged snacks. The point is to strike a balance between getting your family to consume nutrient-dense foods while enjoying their meals. Over time, as you introduce your family to the hidden treasure concept, it will become easier to serve a side of quinoa instead of hiding it in other foods.

Tasty Gem: Foods are considered less whole the more they come in contact with packaging, heat, and people you do not know. Begin reducing the extent to which food is exposed to these elements by consuming more whole foods.

Another dimension to consider when creating a conscious kitchen is what your cooking and storage products are made out of. These products are healthiest if they are made out of recycled material, is recyclable, and the company that makes it strictly follows environmentally and socially responsible business practices. Most nonstick coatings such as Teflon are good to stay away from because they contain artificial chemicals that leech into food. Similarly, plastic spoons, containers, and bags contain such chemicals. Investigate, look for products that are BPA, PTFE and PFOA-free, use materials from nature such as iron skillets and glass bottles, and reuse when possible.

Tasty Gem: Children who eat a diet rich in organically grown food have significantly lower pesticide levels in their bodies, as tested and reflected by blood and urine presence.

Foundational Choices

Making conscious eating choices can feel overwhelming, so it is important to make changes one small step at a time. I have boiled down the general information above to a concise list found below to make this process easier. These suggestions I recommend to all people all the time. Refer back to this list often and begin to make the action steps the foundation of your new eating repertoire. You can even add your own items as you learn more about healthful living. For now, read through the list and decide which choices you are already making and which choices you are willing to implement now and in the future. Pick one area to make a change and get started. Once that item becomes a habit, choose a second area to incorporate into your life. Keep going until you have integrated all that resonate. Foundational eating choices are as follows:

- Eat organically grown food that is locally produced whenever possible.
- Drink, rinse, and cook with filtered water that is free of chemicals such as fluoride, chlorine, and dioxins. My recommendation is https://bit.ly/2tyDXoR.
- Eat whole foods while decreasing the commercially packaged items you purchase.
- Increase your consumption of plant-based and raw food.
- Bake on low temperatures (350 degrees F or below) and avoid cooking the same food multiple times to help your food maintain their nutrient integrity. Foods such as salmon, hemp seeds, and flax seeds contain fragile omega oils and are best cooked below 250 degrees.

- Reduce your use of certain oils, salt, and sweeteners as these stimulate brain centers and can be addictive.
- Look for less processed oils that have gone through cold pressing and are labeled raw or extra-virgin.
- Eat a variety of whole food with different color pigmentations (purple, red, orange, and so forth) on a daily basis but make naturally green food your highest priority.
- Soak oats, grains, nuts, seeds, beans, and legumes in filtered water whenever possible, or purchase presoaked grocery items, to reduce phytic acid, allowing your body to absorb more nutrients and digest food more efficiently.
- Read my blog post to learn more about my Fabulous Favorites for all Things Delicious https://bit.ly/2tlf7K3.

Nutritional Nugget: Health experts from numerous disciplines share the belief that it is not so much "You are what you eat" but rather "You are what you absorb." If your family is eating an organic, healthful diet filled with a diverse range of whole plant-based foods and you are not thriving, then it is time to talk to a trusted holistic food expert about what you can do. It may be that you are not absorbing the nutrients in your food and need to consider gently cleansing the system. It may be that you need to partake in stress-reducing activities or healing work. Most likely, you need to create an overall healthier lifestyle in addition to changing your food habits. A healthy lifestyle includes:

- sleeping in a dark room during the right hours to support recovery and hormone production.
- being asleep earlier. Work your way towards being asleep by 10pm so that your body has enough darkness for optimal hormone production. If this is difficult, start by getting up earlier in the morning, so that you are tired earlier in the evening.
- getting natural light (be outdoors) directly in the eyes for at least 15 minutes per day with a goal of 30 – 60 minutes of outdoor time
- spending quality time in nature
- proper breathing, relaxation and movement
- self-care and pleasurable activities

The list seems long to you. I get it. You don't have to do it alone or all at one time. The good news is I can offer you **effective and result-driven strategies to living a more delicious life** in relation to all these areas. Contact me to claim your free 20 minute Live Deliciously Discovery Session so I can determine how I can help you. Gina@consciouslivingstrategist.com.

The Extra Needed Nutritional Nugget: Almost everyone is deficient in something. It could be vitamin B12, amino acids, omega oils, probiotics, iron, etc. Most likely it is vitamin D as it is very hard to get it from food and most of us aren't making enough in our skin after sun or UV radiation. A deficiency in vitamin D is linked to a whole host of ailments such as obesity, cancer, and arthritis. Dr. Kruse, who I follow, recommends that you get your levels up to between 80 and 100 ng/ml. This is a lot higher than the 35 that is borderline barely okay. What you need to know is that you don't want to be in the normal range but be the optimal range. Most insurance companies will not pay for such a test, so I recommend going online. Check out the D*Action Project that was initiated by 42 leading vitamin D researchers. You can purchase a testing kit at http://www.grassrootshealth.net/daction.

Be gentle with yourself, trust that your body knows how to heal if you give it what it needs, and consider getting support from a coach.

Equipment and Staples Needed

It is extremely helpful to have proper tools and supplies in the kitchen before you set out to make new recipes. Have a quick glance at the recommended items below and compare this to what you have. Keep track of what you discover about your kitchen and begin purchasing or borrowing what you need. Many pieces of equipment can be found at thrift stores and online at sites such as Craigslist. One step at a time begin replacing those items that do not belong in the conscious kitchen you are trying to create.

Recommendations

Small preparation instruments:

1. Wooden cutting board and knives
2. Wooden mixing spoons and spatulas
3. Glass measuring cups and spoons
4. Vegetable peeler
5. Grater
6. Mixing bowls
7. Muslin bag for making nut milk

Tasty Gem: Look for a nut milk bag that is made out of unbleached and organic fabric as materials can leach chemicals into the food they surround.

Cooking instruments and supplies:

1. Pots and pans
2. Baking dishes and pans
3. Muffin and pie pans
4. Cookie sheets
5. Pizza stone (optional)
6. Casserole dishes
7. Glass reusable containers
8. Cloth napkins and organic cotton dish towels
9. Glass or lead-free ceramic glasses and dishes
10. Nontoxic and eco-friendly cleaning products

Tasty Gem: Purchase pots and pans that burn clean and are not coated with toxic chemicals that leech into food especially when heated, such as Teflon.

There are a few big-ticket items that are useful to have when implementing the hidden treasures method. They are:

1. Blender – If you are going to purchase just one large piece of equipment, this is the one to get! I use a Vita-Mix because it has a blade that can puree just about anything, and the company has a few strong ethical guiding principles. However, whatever blender you already have at home should work for the majority of the recipes in this book.
2. Food Processor – This is not absolutely essential if you have a high-powered blender, but it will come in handy.
3. Electric Mix Master or hand-held mixer – Any secondhand brand can work just great.
4. Citrus Squeezer – Great for juicing oranges, lemons, and limes. Electric versions save time and muscle. Non-electric options are cheaper and tend to be more eco-friendly. You can also throw peeled oranges, lemons, and limes in blenders for juicing purposes.
5. Dehydrator (highly recommended but optional as oven instructions are included) – I mostly use an electric dehydrator by Excalibur but am intrigued by a recent discovery, the Food Pantrie. The Food Pantrie has the capacity to hang, removing it from food preparation areas while drying without the use of electricity. They are a lot less expensive and more eco-friendly.

A third option worth mentioning is a solar dehydrator, which dries food by capturing the sun's heat. You can even build your own by looking at videos on the Internet or reviewing the instructions laid out in *The City Homesteader* by Scott Meyer.

Staples

Having the right staples on hand is equally important. Work towards stocking your kitchen with the following items. You may need to ask store managers to order what you need, or you can look at the resource section to learn where to buy these foods online.

Bulk items:
1. Whole grain flours (brown rice, spelt, wheat, and so forth) – preferably sprouted
2. Whole grains (brown rice, millet, bulgur, and so forth) – preferably sprouted
3. Whole pseudograins (amaranth, buckwheat, quinoa, and wild rice)
4. Whole grain pastas, preferably sprouted
5. Himalayan salt and dried spices (pumpkin pie spice and Italian herb)
6. Stevia leaf powder, real maple syrup, and molasses
7. Raw seeds (flax, sesame, pumpkin, sunflower, hemp, and so forth)
8. Raw nuts (cashews, walnuts, brazil, pecans, pistachios, and so forth)
9. Coconut oil and butter
10. Aluminum-free baking powder and soda
11. Raw or extra-virgin olive oil, cold-pressed
12. Dried beans, lentils, and peas
13. Unsulfured dried fruit (raisins, fruit sweetened cranberries, and so forth)
14. Rolled oats
15. Real vanilla extract or vanilla beans
16. Raw nut butters and store-ground peanut butter
17. Unsweetened shredded coconut
18. Buckwheat and oat groats
19. Superfoods – *Moringa oleifera* is the most nutrient-dense of all the superfoods (see resource section for ordering information), and for variety, you may also want to explore maca, chia seeds, chlorella, spirulina, and so forth.
20. Nutritional yeast

Many of the ingredients called for in the following recipes are fresh unpackaged produce that will not keep long and are best used near the time they are harvested when they contain the most nutrients. Some items can be kept frozen (nuts, berries, and so forth) or dehydrated for later use. This is especially helpful if you want to use local organic food after their growing season has ended.

I always have fresh vegetables and fruit on hand and shop a couple a times per week from either our local health food store, the farmer's' market, and/or directly from a local farm. I grow some of my own food from spring until fall, especially those organic items that tend to have the highest price tag. Start by planting items that are the easiest to grow such as tomatoes, potatoes, peas, and strawberries. Each year add an additional growing space with the goal of venturing beyond your comfort zone to grow things that require a bit more attention. Honestly, I am surprised at how easy growing your own food has turned out to be. The trick is to remember to water, make sure that your plants are getting the right amount of sun versus shade, add some rich organic compost to your growing areas each year, and send them a little bit of love every so often. If you find that you are having a problem with bugs or critters, seek the help from a sustainable gardener in your area or call the Seattle Tilth's Garden Hotline at (206) 633-0224. Although based in Seattle, the hotline serves people around the country.

Nutritional Nugget: Eventually you will want to move towards eating less grains and more vegetables. Start by eating whole wheat if you currently eat white breads and pasta. Try switching to sprouted wheat if you already eat whole wheat. Eat less grains if you are living in the gluten free zone (swap carrots and celery sticks for pita when consuming hummus).

Breakfast

It is important to start your day off eating well as it sets the tone for the whole day. One of the best things you can "eat" for breakfast is a green smoothie (fruit, water, and leafy greens). These drinks really fit the bill because they are easy to digest, quick to make, easy to consume on the go, and taste great. Make them part of your morning routine and then consider the other recipes for special occasions when you desire something a bit more savory.

The Superhero Smoothie

Makes 4 servings

Hidden Treasure: plant protein

This is my most popular smoothie because it is basic and tastes great. I think of it as health in a glass but most of my readers say that it is more like dessert in a glass because it tastes so darn good.

4 bananas
6 cups berries (I like to use strawberries and raspberries)
2 packets of Dutch chocolate or vanilla *Moringa oleifera* plant protein*
3 cups water

Combine the bananas, berries, moringa, and water in a high-speed blender, and process until smooth. Stop occasionally to scrape the sides of the blender while moving the mixture towards the blades if needed. Serve immediately and drink slowly.

***Nutritional Nugget**: *Moringa oleifera* is the most nutrient-dense plant discovered. The National Institutes of Health have written about the history of Ayurvedic medicine, which claim that moringa in its best form cures or prevents over 300 ailments.

If you purchase the best variety you will be getting all 20 amino acids. Moringa is important for supplying the essential ones, which our bodies cannot synthesize. These are difficult to find in our food chain today and are critical for health. To purchase the best, the only kind that I will put my name on, go to http://www.ginadiamond.myzija.com/ and select the Enroll button, top right, and search for the plant protein.

Variation: Until you order your moringa you can add 5-10 spinach leaves to the fruit and water listed above and turn it into a green smoothie.

Blueberry-Apple-Banana Smoothie

Makes 4 servings

Hidden Treasure: beet tops

Blueberries and banana are a wonderful combination and they throw off the taste and color of beet tops completely. Begin making this part of your everyday meal plan and work towards drinking a pint (kid) and a quart (adult) daily.

4 bananas
4 cups blueberries
2 apples, chopped
1 ½ cups water
20 red beet tops, torn

Combine the bananas, blueberries, apples, water, and beet tops in a high-speed blender and process until smooth. Stop occasionally to scrape the sides of the blender while moving the mixture towards the blades if needed. Serve immediately and drink slowly.

Nutritional Nugget: Once your family gets used to drinking green smoothies begin adding an additional green leaf every few weeks until you end up with a drink that is half fruit and half vegetables.

Variation: Start by using mild flavored greens such as beet tops or spinach. Later, experiment with greens that have stronger flavors such as kale and collard greens or are a bit more unusual such as miners lettuce and claytonia.

Apple Pie Smoothie

Makes 4 servings

Hidden Treasures: chia seeds and pecans

Cinnamon and the sweetness of apples combine to make a wonderful taste, allowing for a healthful snack or a high-energy dessert. Drink slowly and enjoy apple pie in a glass or slightly warm for an apple cider experience.

4 tablespoons chia seeds
2 cups water
8 sweet apples, chopped
¼ cup pecans
4 teaspoons ground cinnamon
2 teaspoons nutmeg
2 teaspoons dried ginger
1 teaspoon maple syrup (optional)

Put the chia seeds and 4 tablespoons of the water in a small bowl. Mix occasionally until a gel forms, about 10 minutes.

Put the remaining water into a blender. Add the apples, pecans, cinnamon, nutmeg, ginger, maple syrup, and the chia gel. Mix until a liquid is formed and serve immediately.

Hidden Treasure: Maple syrup contains some vitamins and minerals as opposed to table sugar. Like most food, there are different kinds of maple syrup. Look for the pure variety that has no additional ingredients.

Berry-Pear Smoothie

Makes 4 servings

Hidden Treasures: seeds, kale, red pepper, and veggie power

Green smoothies are a must in any healthful diet. The subtle flavor of pear, the sweetness of strawberries and the color of blueberries combine to ensure that children of all ages will eat a dose of vegetables.

1 ½ cups blueberries
10 strawberries with stems intact, sliced
1 pear, sliced
1 tablespoon ground flaxseeds
3 large purple kale leaves
¼ cup chopped red pepper
¼ cup water (optional)

Combine the berries, pear, flax, kale, red pepper, and water in a high-speed blender. Turn on low and gradually work up to full speed. Process until smooth and creamy.

Nutritional Nugget: Sprouting seeds begins the germination process, allowing a dormant seed to become a live plant. This process changes the composition of a seed, stimulating an increase in vitamin content and creating a more digestible end product. Unlike all other seeds, flaxseeds are difficult to sprout at home so a commercial process is preferred.

Melon Smoothie

Makes 4 servings

Hidden Treasure: lettuce

The beautiful color and sweet taste of melon hides the greens beautifully. Place a mint leaf on top for a fancier look and enjoy at a party.

1 large honeydew melon, chopped
4 large green lettuce leaves
½ teaspoon spirulina powder (optional)

Combine the melon, lettuce, and spirulina in a high-speed blender, and process until smooth. Serve immediately and drink slowly.

Nutritional Nugget: Spirulina is a blue-green algae that is considered to be a complete protein and contains a long list of vitamins and minerals. Make sure the company that harvests the spirulina you purchase tests for algae contamination and supplies the purest algae available.

Variation: Replace ½ teaspoon of spirulina powder with ½ teaspoon of any organic green powder.

Persimmon Smoothie

Makes 4 servings

Hidden Treasures: seeds, red pepper, and spinach

If you want to expand your horizons begin trying new fruits in your smoothies. Persimmons are sweet and delicious and irresistible to children and adults alike. They provide a great cover for hidden treasures that kids may not normally choose to eat and often can be found in stores in the fall months.

14 persimmons
6 tablespoons hemp seeds
½ red pepper, chopped
5 red spinach leaves

Combine the persimmons, seeds, pepper, and spinach in a high-speed blender and process until smooth. Stop occasionally to scrape the sides of the blender while moving the mixture towards the blades if needed. Serve immediately and drink slowly.

Nutritional Nugget: Persimmons are a type of fruit that are rich in health-promoting benefits because they contain vitamins A, B, and C, phytonutrients, and minerals such as manganese and potassium. They are usually in season in the fall.

Granola

Makes 10 servings

Hidden Treasures: walnuts, seeds, and cauliflower

This granola's sweet taste is subtle and can be eaten right out of the jar or in a bowl with non-dairy milk or yogurt. It makes a wonderful after-school snack or an energy-boosting treat on family walks through the woods. Your kids might just disappear with it and return from their room with an empty bowl.

5 cups rolled oats
½ cup walnuts
½ cup almonds
1 cup cauliflower florets
½ cup pumpkin seeds
½ cup sunflower seeds
½ cup sesame seeds
½ cup ground flaxseeds
⅓ cup maple syrup or coconut palm sugar
⅓ cup extra virgin olive oil
1–2 cups dried fruit such as raisins, cranberries, or apples (the more fruit the more dense this recipe becomes)

Preheat the oven to 300 degrees F.

Spread the oats evenly onto a cookie sheet. Put the sheet in the oven and cook for 15 minutes, stirring halfway through. While the oats are cooking, pulse-grind the walnuts, almonds, cauliflower, pumpkin, sunflower, and sesame seeds in a food processor until the nuts are undetectable.

Take the oats out of the oven and put them in a large bowl. Add the nut mixture, sugar, and oil. Mix well. Add the dried fruit and serve cold. Put in a large glass jar with a tight lid for storage. Granola will keep for several months at room temperature.

Nutritional Nugget: Coconut palm sugar comes in the form of crystals or nectar. It is said to have a naturally low glycemic index and contains some micronutrients, such as potassium. Make sure you purchase 100% pure organic coconut palm sugar and use it sparingly because it is still sugar. It can be used to replace maple syrup in any of my recipes.

Variation: For a crunchier taste, cook the granola for an additional 25 minutes in a 250 degree F oven before the fruit is added. Stir once while baking. Remove the granola from the oven, cool completely, and add the dried fruit. Put in a large glass jar with a tight lid for storage. Granola will keep for several months.

Wholesome Pancakes

Makes 4 servings

Hidden Treasures: flaxseeds and kale

These pancakes are the perfect morning meal for a special event such as Father's Day. The kale is very subtle and mixes well with the pancake mix. Top with sliced strawberries, a sprinkling of ground flaxseeds, and a drizzle of maple syrup.

4 tablespoons ground flaxseeds
8 tablespoons water
3 cups whole grain flour
3 teaspoons baking powder
3 ¼ cups "Plant a Seed" Milk (page 34)
2 teaspoons vanilla extract
½ cup kale

Put the flaxseeds and water in a small bowl and stir occasionally until a gel forms.

In a medium bowl, mix the flour with baking powder and set aside. Combine the flaxseed mixture, milk, and vanilla in a second medium bowl. Slowly add the liquid mixture into the flour mixture, stirring constantly.

Put the greens in a food processor and finely chop. Scrape the greens out of the processor and fold them into the flour mix.

Coat a pan with coconut oil and ladle small mounds of dough onto the pan and cook over medium-low heat. Flip the pancake after 1 minute, press down on the cooked side, and let the dough expand. Cook the pancake for a 2 more minutes and flip again. After another minute place the cooked cake into an oven and turn the heat to 200 degrees F. Repeat this process until all the batter is used. Enjoy immediately or store in the refrigerator for 2–4 days for later use.

Gina D. Diamond, M.Ed.

Banana-Oat Pancakes

Makes 4 servings

Hidden Treasures: chia seeds, quinoa, cauliflower, and almonds

The taste of oats and bananas, combined with almond milk, vanilla, and maple syrup will put smiles on your family members' faces. Add sliced bananas on top and eat up!

2 tablespoons chia seeds
6 tablespoons water
½ cup minced cauliflower
3 cups whole wheat flour
½ cup rolled oats
2 teaspoons baking soda
½ cup cooked quinoa
1 large ripe banana
2 cups Nut Milk (page 33) or unsweetened store-bought option
2 teaspoons vanilla extract
2 tablespoons maple syrup

Mix the chia seeds and water in a small bowl. Set aside until a gel forms.

Put the cauliflower in a food processor and pulse-chop until the pieces are fine. Mix flour, oats, baking soda, quinoa, and cauliflower together in a medium bowl. Set aside.

Mash the banana in a separate medium bowl. Stir in the chia mixture, nut milk, vanilla, and maple syrup. Pour the flour mixture into the banana mixture and stir with a wooden spoon until all the ingredients blend together.

Put a large spoonful of the mixture on a well-oiled skillet on a medium burner. Cook on one side until lightly brown. Flip and cook on the other side until the pancake scrapes off easily. Put the pancakes in a low-heat oven until the last one is made. Serve immediately with your favorite toppings.

Tasty Gem: Cook a large amount of quinoa and use the leftovers to make Date-Banana Balls (page 118). Also, add more oil to the skillet between each pancake battering.

Fabulous French Toast

Makes 4 servings

Hidden Treasures: squash and seeds

Enjoy this healthful version of French toast, which calls for fruit and coconut milk instead of egg and dairy. The finished product is a little lighter than traditional toasts yet it still maintains its sweet and hearty taste.

8 pieces whole grain bread
4 small ripe bananas
1 cup Coconut Magic Milk (page 35) or any unsweetened store-bought nut milk
½ cup finely grated yellow squash
2 teaspoons ground cinnamon
1 teaspoon vanilla extract
Garnish with ground flaxseeds and strawberry slices

Dry out the bread to avoid soggy French toast by laying the slices on a cookie sheet overnight.

Put the bananas, coconut milk, squash, cinnamon, and vanilla in a high-speed blender, process until smooth. Pour the banana mixture into a pie pan. Dip each side of the bread slices into the batter before placing into a lightly oiled large pan. Cook 2 pieces at a time; warm one side over medium-low heat for 2 minutes and then flip, warming the other side for 2 minutes. Put the cooked slices in a 150 degree F oven until the batch is completed. Remove from the oven and sprinkle with the flaxseeds and top with strawberry slices. Serve warm.

Nutritional Nugget: Flaxseeds contain omega fatty acids that can be destroyed by heat. Avoid cooking flaxseeds, or warm below 300 degree F.

Kid Crepes

Makes 36 servings

Hidden Treasures: seeds, oat groats, and zucchini

Sweet crepes are particularly good for dessert but this recipe works well for breakfast because they are mostly bananas. They are light but filling, and even the pickiest eaters ask for them. Add Banana Soft Serve (page 112) and Cashew Cream (page 53) to turn these crepes into a special meal for Mother's Day.

25 ripe bananas
1 cup ground flaxseeds
1 cup oat groats, soaked
1 small zucchini, chopped

Put the bananas, seeds, groats, and zucchini in a blender. Turn the blender on low and mix for 30 seconds. Slowly increase the speed, stopping to scrape the sides of the blender if necessary. Blend until a creamy and smooth mixture is achieved.

Put four ¼ cup mounds of mixture on each dehydrator sheet and spread with a spoon until the mixture is thinned but the sheet is not visible. Dehydrate at 105 degrees for approximately 8 hours. Check the leathers after 7 hours, removing them as soon as they are ready. Scrape them off easily by using the flat edge of a knife or a clean fingernail. Place in a tightly covered container and store at room temperature. Crepes will last one month.

Nutritional Nugget: Oat groats are the kernel that oats are derived from. They contain vitamins E and B, a whole host of minerals, and fiber.

Variation: Instead of using a dehydrator, cook crepes on a baking sheet coated with coconut oil for 15 minutes in a 250 degree oven.

Beverages

It is very easy to put hidden treasures in drinks, especially if you have a high-speed blender and can mix the ingredients until the pieces become undetectable. Regular blenders do not always have the capacity to create smooth drinks, so you may need to tweak the recipes until you can borrow or purchase a heavy-duty version. Aside from drinks, you can use a high-speed blender to make creamy recipes such as soups, ice cream, spreads, and more. Start with the drinks as they are simple and quick to make. They are quite refreshing on warm days and are great to consume while exercising.

Oranger Julius

Makes 4 servings

Hidden Treasures: probiotics, seeds, and celery

This is a refreshing drink that can be enjoyed all year round. It tastes similar to the classic Orange Julius you may remember from your last trip to the mall but with healthful ingredients.

4 medium juice oranges, peeled and quartered
3 cups plain coconut yogurt or soy yogurt
1 cup "Plant a Seed" Milk (page 34)
4 teaspoons vanilla extract
2 teaspoons maple syrup
½ cup celery, minced
4 cups ice (optional)

Put the oranges, yogurt, milk, vanilla, syrup, celery, and ice into a blender and process until the drink is smooth and frothy. Serve immediately.

Nutritional Nugget: The white coating between the skin and the fruit on citrus is called the pith. It contains lots of fiber and vitamin C so I like to include it in my recipes when possible.

Gina D. Diamond, M.Ed.

Wonderful Watermelon Delight

Makes 4 servings

Hidden Treasure: jicama

Look for local watermelon in the warmer months and make this drink to cool your family off. Ask the store manager to help you pick out a sweet melon and then go home to make this simple and delicious drink.

¼ cup jicama, chopped
1 medium watermelon, chopped

Put the jicama and watermelon into a high-speed blender and mix well. Serve at room temperature or add ice for a colder beverage.

Nutritional Nugget: Jicama is a root vegetable and a great source of dietary fiber, rich in vitamin C, and has small amounts of B-complex vitamins and minerals. It is sweet, crunchy, and delicious all on its own.

Nut Milk

Makes 4 servings

Hidden Treasure: almonds

Consume nut milk by itself or use it as a base for smoothies, sauces, and Popsicles. Homemade milk is the best because it is less processed, less money, and much more nutritious.

2 cups almonds
4 cups water, plus more as needed
1 teaspoon vanilla extract (optional)
2 teaspoons stevia leaf powder (optional)

Put the almonds into a bowl and cover with half of the water. Soak in the refrigerator for at least 8 hours.

Collect the bowl of nuts from the refrigerator and pour the water into an empty jar and use to water your plants. Rinse the nuts, put them in a blender with the remaining water and optional vanilla and stevia. Mix on high until a thick liquid is formed.

Using a cloth nut bag and a pitcher with a large open rim, separate the liquid from the fiber. Reserve the nut fiber to replace some of the flour in your favorite recipes or use as a bath scrub. Cover the liquid (nut milk) with a clean cloth and store in the refrigerator for 5–7 days. Stir the milk before serving, as the nuts and water will separate.

Nutritional Nuggets: Look for 100% pure stevia leaf powder that is green, not white. The green powder is the natural green leaf ground into powder, not an extract. This powder has been found to contain over 100 phytonutrients, which are compounds found in plants that have a number of beneficial attributes including boosting the immune system.

The U.S. law that passed requiring almonds to be pasteurized is still in effect. However, there are a few loopholes. See the resource section to inquire.

Gina D. Diamond, M.Ed.

"Plant a Seed" Milk

Makes 4 servings

Hidden Treasure: seeds

This drink has a soft texture and a subtle taste. It is wonderful on a bowl of Granola (page 23).

2 cup hemp seeds or sunflower seeds
2 cups water
2 cups Date Water (page 40)
1 teaspoon vanilla extract (optional)

Put the seeds into a bowl and cover with half of the water. Soak in the refrigerator for at least 8 hours.

Collect the bowl of seeds and pour the water into an empty jar and use to water your plants. Rinse the seeds and put them in a blender with the remaining water, Date Water, and vanilla. Mix on high until a thick liquid is formed. Put the seeds, water, and vanilla into a blender. Mix on high until a milk consistency is achieved.

Pour the blended mixture into a nut bag. The edges of the nut bag should be folded over a pitcher that has a wide opening. Let the liquid drip for two minutes. Hold the cloth above the pitcher and twist, squeezing gently until all of the liquid is released. Cover the pitcher with a clean cloth and store in the refrigerator for 5–7 days. Stir the milk before serving, as the seeds and water will separate.

Nutritional Nugget: Hemp seeds are a great source of complete protein and essential fats and are so much easier for humans to digest than dairy.

Coconut Magic Milk

Makes 4 servings

Hidden Treasures: coconut and seeds

Organic coconut milk is available in stores but it often comes in a tin can lined with Bisphenol A (BPA), a toxic plastic chemical that can leach into food. This recipe is offered as an alternative to store-bought options because you can avoid tin cans altogether. It is really easy to make with only a few ingredients. You can drink it with cookies, add to soups, or replace in recipes anytime dairy milk is called for.

4 cups water
1 cup coconut manna or coconut butter
1 tablespoon hemp seeds (optional)

Put a jar of the manna in a pot of water so that it is partially submerged. Bring the water to a very low simmer and gently warm until the manna is runny. Put the liquid manna, hempseeds, and water in a high-speed blender for 10 seconds. Enjoy in any recipe that calls for coconut milk such as Mouth-Watering Mashed Potatoes (page 81).

Tasty Gem: Look for organic coconut manna that comes in a glass bottle or in a plastic container marked with #1 on the bottom. Plastics designated with the #1 are safer for one time use as compared to many other plastics.

Gina D. Diamond, M.Ed.

Ginger-Strawberry Lemonade

Makes 4 servings

Hidden Treasures: ginger and strawberry hulls

Ginger is wonderful as it soothes the intestinal track, and the lemon and strawberries add life and taste to this important root plant. It is great for kids because it isn't too tart or too sweet.

6 cups water
1 cup freshly squeezed lemon juice
1 tablespoon maple syrup
½ teaspoon fresh ginger
8 strawberries, dehulled
ice cubes (optional)

Put the water, juice, syrup, ginger, and strawberries into a blender. Mix well. Serve immediately before the ingredients settle. Add ice cubes if a cooler temperature is desired.

Full Speed Ahead Chocolate Milk

Makes 4 servings

Hidden Treasures: dates and green powder

This drink is wonderful any time of the year but it is especially nice when it is served warm on a snowy day. Serve as a special treat, reserve it for a healthful dessert, or pour over quinoa for some added nutrition.

4 cups Coconut Magic Milk (page 35) or store-bought option
5 tablespoons cocoa powder
20 large pitted dates, soaked
1 teaspoon green powder (optional)
½ teaspoon vanilla extract (optional)
½ teaspoon ground cinnamon (optional)
4 mint leaves (optional)

Put the milk, cocoa, dates, green powder, vanilla, cinnamon, and mint into a blender and process until smooth. Pour into glasses and drink immediately or warm slightly by processing for 2 additional minutes in the blender.

Nutritional Nugget: The green that I like to use in this recipe is chlorella. Chlorella is an edible green algae that can detoxify the body, improve immune system function, and increase energy levels. It contains protein, magnesium, carotenoids, and B12. Gradually increase the amount of chlorella each time you serve this drink until you reach 5 tablespoons. Make sure the company that harvests the chlorella you purchase tests for algae contamination and supplies the purest algae available.

Variation: Replace the cocoa and green powder with Moringa *oleifera* Dutch chocolate protein powder (to purchase, see Suppliers at the end of this section).

Mint Milkshake

Makes 4 servings

Hidden Treasures: almonds, mint, and avocado

This drink can serve as a healthful snack as it only contains fruit sugars. However, since it is so sweet and creamy, it can easily pass for dessert. The fresh taste of mint combined with the sweet taste of dates and bananas makes for a delicious milkshake.

4 cups Nut Milk (page 33) or unsweetened store-bought option
4 large pitted dates, soaked
1 cup fresh mint leaves, loosely packed
2 frozen ripe bananas
1 teaspoon vanilla extract
½ avocado
2 teaspoons green superfood powder (optional)
2 ice cubes (optional)
Garnish with mint leaves

Put the milk, dates, mint, bananas, vanilla, avocado, green powder, and ice cubes into a blender and process until smooth. Serve immediately or put in the freezer for a later use.

Nutritional Nugget: Look for a green superfood powder that is organic and comes from a company that you trust. You can purchase powders online at a variety of sites or in many natural food stores.

Mango Lassi

Makes 4 – 6 servings

Hidden Treasures: probiotics, cucumber, and mint

The yogurt, cucumber, and mango combined make this drink creamy, refreshing, sweet, and a healthier version than that which you find in most Indian restaurants. Try making it with unsweetened yogurt and if you are not able, enjoy this as a delicious dessert.

2 large ripe mangos, sliced
3 cups plain coconut yogurt or non-GMO soy yogurt
1 cup water
¼ cucumber, sliced
4 mint sprigs
4 ice cubes (optional)

Put the mangos, yogurt, water, cucumber, mint, and ice in a high-speed blender. Slowly turn the machine from low to high. Process until smooth and pour the mixture into 4 separate bowls. Put in the refrigerator until ready to serve.

Nutritional Nuggets: The probiotics in the yogurt will help aid gastrointestinal health by maintaining the natural balance of microflora. Also, look for 100% pure stevia leaf powder. The green powder is the natural green leaf ground into powder, not an extract. This powder has been found to contain over 100 phytonutrients, which are compounds found in plants that have a number of beneficial attributes including boosting the immune system.

Date Water

Makes 4 servings

Hidden Treasures: dates

Date water is great for kids who refuse to drink water. Its sweet, subtle taste makes it very versatile. Use it to replace water and sugar in recipes such as lemonade or in desserts such as ice cream.

4 cups water
20 large pitted dates

Put the water and dates into a bowl. Let the dates sit for 1–3 hours, depending on the desired sweetness. Strain the dates and put them in the refrigerator for future use in baked goods or fruit leathers and reserve the water for drinking.

Halftime Drink

Makes 2 servings

Hidden Treasures: dulse and coconut

Looking to get some electrolytes in your sports drink naturally? This recipe is a healthful alternative to Gatorade without all the harmful ingredients. Your kids can enjoy this drink at halftime during their big game or sip during a long bike ride.

3 soaked dates, chopped
1 teaspoon dulse flakes
2 cups water
1 tablespoon coconut nectar or maple syrup
2 teaspoons carob powder
1 tablespoon diced mint leaves
1 teaspoon coconut oil
Sea salt, to taste

Combine the dates, dulse, water, nectar, carob powder, mint, oil, and salt in a high-speed blender. Process until smooth and consume slowly.

Nutritional Nugget: Dulse is a sea vegetable that contains over 100 minerals and trace elements. It is also known for hydrating the body.

Reprinted by permission from *Thrive* by Brendan Brazier (Philadelphia, PA: Da Capo Press, 2008).

Variation: You can also purchase a store-bought version through my business, as there is finally a 100% truly natural energy drink. Go to www.ginadiamond.myzija.com, select Enroll in the top right corner, and search for the Ripstix fitness line.

Salad Dressings, Sauces, and Spreads

Salad dressings, sauces, and spreads can go with just about anything, so serve them with any recipe that calls for additional flavor. They are interchangeable and wonderful to have in the refrigerator for the times when you need a quick healthful snack or light meal. Reserve half of a Sunday to make a couple recipes and serve them to your family for a ready-to-eat meal or after-school feast.

Mac Cream Dressing

Makes 4 servings

Hidden Treasures: macadamia nuts, cauliflower, and bee pollen

For some kids the dressing or dip is the appeal to eating vegetables. This is a raw, whole foods recipe that may just encourage your family to eat more salads. Eat with a side of veggies or add to soups to create a thicker consistency and a tangier taste.

1 cup macadamia nuts
¼ cup water
⅓ cup extra virgin olive oil
¼ cup freshly squeezed lemon juice
1 tablespoon apple cider vinegar
3 dates, soaked
3 garlic cloves
1 tablespoon onion flakes
½ teaspoon salt
½ cup cauliflower florets
½ tablespoon bee pollen (optional)
1 teaspoon dill (optional)

Cover the macadamia nuts with water and soak for 2 hours. Drain and rinse.

Put the soaked nuts, water, oil, lemon juice, vinegar, dates, garlic, onion flakes, salt, cauliflower, and bee pollen into a blender and process until smooth. Transfer the dressing to a quart glass jar with a lid and stir in the dill. Put in the refrigerator to thicken and serve when ready. This dressing will keep for 7 - 10 days.

Nutritional Nugget: Bee pollen has a sweet taste and can help eliminate seasonal allergies when ingested. Bee pollen has over 96 nutrients and is often called nature's most perfect food. Use caution if you have a bee allergy, and make sure you know your source as pollen is used as an air-quality indicator and can absorb pollution.

Tomato-Lime Dressing

Makes 4 servings

Hidden Treasures: lime, celery, miso, and herbs

The tomato and lime combine to make a light, refreshing taste that is tangy and unusual. It goes great with a salad fresh from the garden, can be served slightly warm on top of toasted bread, or drizzled over quinoa.

6 cups chopped tomato
3 limes, peeled and chopped
3 cups chopped celery
3 tablespoons chickpea miso paste
3 teaspoons Italian seasoning

Put the tomatoes, limes, celery, miso, and seasoning into a blender and process until smooth. Serve immediately or transfer to a quart glass jar for storage. This dressing will keep for 14 days in the back of your refrigerator.

Variation: Replace 3 tablespoons of the chickpea miso paste with 3 tablespoons of brown rice miso.

Perky Pesto

Makes 4 servings

Hidden Treasures: herbs, nettles, seeds, and zucchini

This spread goes great on pasta, on top of lentils, or as a side dish. The basil disguises all the hidden treasures and works well for those who are used to eating traditional pesto.

⅔ cup pumpkin seeds
1– 4 garlic cloves
3 cups loosely packed fresh basil
1 cup loosely packed dried nettles
½ cup zucchini, chopped
½ cup extra virgin olive oil
1 teaspoon salt
2 tablespoons sesame seeds (optional)

Cover the pumpkin seeds with water and soak for 8 hours. Discard the water, rinse the seeds with water, and pour into a food processor with the garlic, basil, nettles, zucchini, oil, and salt and seeds. Mix well by using pulse-chop setting.

Heat the pesto in a medium skillet over low heat if you desire a mild taste or serve raw. Place pesto in a glass jar with a tight lid and keep in the back of your refrigerator for 14 days.

Nutritional Nugget: Nettles are an herb that can be foraged in the spring, purchased at farmers' markets, and available online in powder form. They have a high mineral and protein content.

Variation: Replace 1 cup dried nettles with 1 cup bok choy or kale leaves if the nettles are difficult to find.

Notes: Thin needles coat the stem and leaves of the nettle plant. Always wear gloves when handling raw nettles and make sure that you cook or dry them before eating. To dry nettles, simply lay them on a paper grocery bag and leave out to dry. When the leaves and needles shrivel, they are ready to eat.

Gina D. Diamond, M.Ed.

Apple Sauce

Makes 4 servings

Hidden Treasures: seeds

Apple sauce makes for a healthful snack, a tasty side dish, or a comforting wholesome treat. Serve warm with Lively Latkes (see page 73) or over ice cream to add flavor and nutrients.

8 small dates
3 sweet apples, chopped and cored
1 cup water, plus more for soaking
2 teaspoons hemp seeds or ground flaxseeds
1 teaspoon ground cinnamon

Halve and pit the dates. Put them into a bowl, cover with water, and soak for 5–10 minutes.

Put the dates, half of the apples, water, and hemp seeds in a high-speed blender and puree until smooth and slightly warm. Put the remaining apples and cinnamon in the blender and mix on low to create a chunky and inviting applesauce. Serve immediately.

Nutritional Nugget: Hemp seeds are a great source of complete protein and essential fats.

Ketchup

Makes 12 servings

Hidden Treasures: dates, red pepper, and seeds

Commercial ketchups usually contain a large amount of sugar and are heavily processed. You can make your own quite easily, and this recipe tastes fresher and has a higher nutrient volume than the store-bought options.

1 large red tomato, chopped
1 cup sundried tomatoes, soaked
6 large dried dates, soaked
¼ cup extra virgin olive oil
¼ cup chopped red pepper
2 tablespoons apple cider vinegar
1 tablespoon water
1 teaspoon ground flaxseeds
1 teaspoon sea salt
1 clove garlic (optional)

Put the tomatoes, dates, oil, red pepper, vinegar, water, flaxseeds, water and salt in a food processor and blend until smooth. Stored in a glass jar in the refrigerator, the ketchup will keep for 2-4 weeks.

Nutritional Nugget: Consider growing or purchasing organic heirloom tomatoes to use in this recipe. Heirloom varieties are grown from seeds that are handed down from generation to generation. Compared to modern hybrid seeds, they produce food that is more nutritious and often tastier.

Variation: Replace 2 tablespoons of vinegar with 2 tablespoons of freshly squeezed lemon juice

Powerful Pink Sauce

Makes 4 servings

Hidden Treasures: cashew butter, mushrooms, onion, garlic, and nori

This pink sauce is very versatile. It can be eaten raw over pasta made from zucchini stripes or cooked and used as a pizza sauce. It is especially delicious warm over sprouted whole grain pasta or Vegetable-Rice Pie (page 71).

5 roma tomatoes
2 tablespoons cashew butter
1 tablespoon tomato paste (can use remainder in chili, shepherd's pie, or on pizza crust)
2 teaspoons Italian seasoning
1 tablespoon diced red onion
½ clove garlic
3 tablespoons water
¼ sheet nori, untoasted (optional)
½ teaspoon salt (optional)

Cut 2 tomatoes into cubes. Set aside. Put the remaining tomatoes into a blender with the cashew butter, tomato paste, seasoning, red onion, garlic, water, and nori. Blend well. Pour the sauce into a pan and add the remaining tomatoes. Cook on a medium-low heat for 30 minutes, stirring occasionally. The sauce is ready to serve when it is thick and juicy.

Nutritional Nugget: Nori is a high- nutrient sea vegetable that contains protein, vitamin C, folate, iodine, iron, and calcium. Look for seaweed that has been harvested from the wild, not farmed.

Variation: Once your kids agree that they like this sauce, try it over some spaghetti squash to challenge their taste buds and open them up to new possibilities.

Raw Red Marinara

Makes 8 servings

Hidden Treasures: ginger, garlic, herbs, and red pepper

This wonderful marinara sauce is so good that you can eat it by itself. However, most prefer to use it in lasagna recipes, smothered over spaghetti squash, or drizzled on top of zucchini noodles. Thank you for sharing, Cherie Calbom.

½ cup pineapple, chopped
2 cups tomatoes, chopped
1 teaspoon fresh ginger
2 tablespoons garlic, minced
⅓ cup fresh basil leaves, chopped and packed, or 2 tablespoons dried
¼ cup chopped red bell pepper
⅓ cup sundried tomatoes, soaked
⅓ cup fresh oregano leaves, de-stemmed and chopped, or 2 tablespoons dried
1 ½ teaspoons sea salt, preferably Celtic
1 cup extra virgin olive oil
1 teaspoon jalapeño minced (optional)

Blend all ingredients together in a food processor. Remove and store in a quart mason jar. Set the sauce in the refrigerator for at least an hour so it will thicken and become more flavorful.

Fruit Dip

Makes 4 serving

Hidden Treasures: beets, walnuts, and seeds

Fruit dip has a multitude of purposes and is extremely easy to make. You can eat it like yogurt, serve it with fruit, or use it to top a dessert such as Brownies (page 122) or meal such as Fabulous French Toast (page 27).

¼ cup whole walnuts
⅛ cup red beet
7 ripe strawberries, sliced
1 ripe banana
¼ cup creamed coconut or coconut butter
1 tablespoon ground flaxseeds

Put the walnuts, beets, berries, banana, coconut, and flaxseeds in a food processor and grind until a smooth dip is formed. Pour the mixture into a small bowl and put it into the refrigerator. This dip will last 7 days.

Nutritional Nugget: Remember to leave strawberry stems on for extra minerals and chlorophyll, and be sure to use the reddest berries for a sweeter taste.

Cashew Cream Cheese Spread

Makes 4 servings

Hidden Treasures: cashews and cauliflower

Nut cheese can be a bit sophisticated for some kids, but those who like cream cheese and hummus will probably go for it. Enjoy this smooth spread with fresh veggies or sprouted whole grain crackers.

2 cups cashews
1 small lemon, peeled and chopped
½ cup ground cauliflower
2 large cloves garlic
1 ½ teaspoons sea salt
¾ cup extra virgin olive oil
¼ cup water

Cover the cashews with water and soak for 8 hours. Discard the water, rinse the nuts with water, and pour into a high-speed blender.

Add the lemon, cauliflower, garlic, salt, olive oil, and water. Blend the ingredients on low until all the ingredients are mixed, scraping the sides of the blender as needed. Slowly turn the blender to high and blend for an additional 30 seconds until a cream cheese consistency is formed. It is always best to eat food as soon as possible and this spread will store in a quart mason jar in the refrigerator for maximum 7 -10 days.

Gina D. Diamond, M.Ed.

Sunflower Pate

Makes 4 servings

Hidden Treasures: seeds, bok choy, garlic, and lemon

The sunflower seeds in this recipe have a very subtle taste, which makes for a nice dipping sauce for those picky eaters. Add to soups to thicken and enliven your recipes or use as a great mayonnaise substitute. Delicious indeed!

2 cups sunflower seeds
⅔ cup fresh lemon juice (about 2 medium lemons)
Scant ⅔ cup extra virgin olive oil
⅔ cups water, plus more for soaking
3 medium garlic cloves
¼ cup bok choy, leaves removed (about 2 stalks)
2 teaspoons sea salt

Cover the seeds with water and soak for 8 hours. Discard the water, rinse the seeds with water, and pour into a high-speed blender.

Add the juice, oil, water, garlic, bok choy, and salt. Blend the ingredients on low until all the ingredients are mixed. Slowly turn the blender to high and blend for an additional 30 seconds. Store the spread in a quart mason in the refrigerator for 7 to 10 days.

Nutritional Nugget: Reserved bok choy leaves can be blended into a smoothie.

Extra-Green Guacamole

Makes 4 servings

Hidden Treasures: asparagus and hemp seeds

Guacamole is often a favorite at parties. This version tastes great, is lighter than most, and offers some additional nutrients that traditional recipes omit. If the asparagus taste is too strong for your picky eaters, you can lightly steam these veggies for a milder taste or leave them out altogether. Serve with raw vegetables.

½ cup chopped asparagus spears, trimmed
1 tablespoon hemp seeds (optional)
2 avocados
2 tablespoons fresh lemon juice
1 teaspoon salt
½ small tomato, finely chopped (optional)
1 tablespoon minced cilantro (optional)

Put the asparagus and seeds in a food processor and blend into a paste. Scoop the avocado into a bowl and add the asparagus mixture, juice, and salt. Mash until a few avocado chunks remain. Add the tomato and cilantro and mix well.

Guacamole tastes best when it is fresh but it will keep for 2 days if stored in a glass container with a tight lid in the refrigerator.

Tasty Gem: Placing one of the discarded avocado pits in the guacamole will keep it from turning brown.

Gina D. Diamond, M.Ed.

Hyped-up Hummus

Makes 4 servings

Hidden Treasures: sunchoke, chickpeas, and tahini

Hummus is a favorite amongst old and young. It is hearty enough to eat as a meal with a plate full of Vegetable Crackers (page 98), or try it with sprouted whole grain pita bread accompanied by a soup or salad. I really love it for a quick, hearty on-the-go snack.

1 cup cooked or canned chickpeas
½ cup sunchoke, chopped
¼ cup fresh lemon juice
¼ cup water
3 tablespoons tahini
2 tablespoons extra-virgin olive oil
1 large garlic clove
½ teaspoon salt
½ teaspoon ground cumin (optional)

Put the chickpeas in a high-speed blender. Add the sunchoke, lemon juice, water, tahini, oil, garlic, salt, and cumin and blend until creamy. Store in an airtight container in the refrigerator. The hummus will last 7-10 days.

Nutritional Nuggets: A sunchoke, also called a Jerusalem artichoke, contains vitamin C, phosphorus, potassium, and iron, as well as inulin, which promotes good intestinal health. Also, tahini is made from ground up sesame seeds and is packed full of B vitamins and calcium.

Burgers and Soups

Burgers and soups are entrées with wonderful hidden treasures because healthful ingredients are barely detectable amongst these meals that are commonly eaten by children. The following recipes yield large serving sizes so your efforts go a long way. Get creative by mixing and matching these meals with a variety of sides to keep your family from getting bored.

Garden Burgers

Makes 12 servings

Hidden Treasures: oat groats, carrots, spinach, and parsley

Burgers are great smothered in Ketchup (page 49) with a side of Veggie Fries (page 85) and a salad. The trick to any garden burger is to flip it halfway through the cooking process to ensure that it forms a crispy crust on both sides.

1 cup whole oat groats
3 cups plus 3 tablespoons water
1 tablespoon ground flaxseeds
1 large carrot, chopped
3 large spinach leaves
2 tablespoons fresh chopped parsley
½ teaspoon sea salt

Combine groats and 3 cups of the water in a pan, cover, and bring to a boil. Reduce the heat to low and simmer until the groats are tender, 45–60 minutes. Drain the water, let the groats cool, and set aside.

Combine the flaxseeds and 3 tablespoons of water, stirring occasionally until a gel forms. Put the prepared oat groats, carrots, spinach, parsley, salt, and flax mixture in a blender and blend until a coarse texture is achieved.

Preheat the oven to 300 degrees F. While the oven is warming, form the mixture into patties and place on a lightly coated cookie sheet. Bake for 30 minutes, flipping once half-way through.

Nutritional Nugget: Oat groats are the kernels that oats are derived from. They contain vitamins E and B, a whole host of minerals, and fiber.

Tasty Gem: Soak the groats in water to cut down on cooking time.

Farro Burgers

Makes 12 servings

Hidden Treasures: farro, sunflower seeds, and vegetables

This recipe is one of my absolute favorites. It lends itself to a hearty meal and is especially pleasurable to eat when it is cold outside. It bakes to a nice crisp and goes great with Ketchup (page 49) and a side serving of Green Chips (page 84).

1 ½ cups farro berries
¼ cup finely diced sweet onion
⅛ cup soy sauce
2 garlic gloves, minced
½ tablespoon Italian herb seasoning
3 cups water, plus more for soaking
½ cup sunflower seeds, ground if a hidden option is more desirable
1 cup shredded vegetables such as carrots, squash, zucchini, and broccoli

Cover the farro berries with water and soak for 8 hours. Drain and rinse the berries. Put berries in a high-speed blender and grind until only specks of grain are visible.

Lightly oil a pot with coconut oil and cook the onions, soy sauce, garlic, and seasoning on medium-low heat, stirring occasionally, until the onions become translucent. Add the water to the onion mixture and bring to a slow boil. Reduce the heat to low and add the farro. Simmer the mixture for 5 minutes, stirring frequently. Remove the pot from the burner and add the seeds and vegetables. Continue stirring occasionally until the farro mixture becomes thick. Let the mixture cool.

Form the mixture into patties and place them on a lightly oiled baking sheet. Bake for 35–45 minutes at 300 degrees F, flipping half-way through.

Nutritional Nugget: Farro is a whole grain that is high in fiber, protein, and antioxidants.

Zucchini Patties

Makes 12 servings

Hidden Treasures: chickpeas, zucchini, onion, and red pepper

The breadcrumbs in this recipe taste great and wonderfully mask the hidden treasures. They are best consumed in moderation so eat them only occasionally and with lots of other foods that are nutrient dense. Serve with chunks of Kabocha squash and a salad.

½ cup cooked chickpeas
2 cups water
1 medium zucchini
½ cup fresh or thawed corn
¼ cup red pepper, diced
2 teaspoons minced onion
1 teaspoon soy sauce
½ teaspoon Italian seasoning
1 ½ cups whole grain breadcrumbs

Put the chickpeas and zucchini in a food processor and blend until they turn into a coarse paste.

Put the mixture in a medium bowl and stir in the corn, pepper, onion, soy sauce, seasoning, and breadcrumbs. Form the mixture into patties. Place the patties on a lightly oiled cookie sheet and bake for 15 to 20 minutes on each side at 300 degrees F.

Nutritional Nuggets: Kabocha squash is very sweet, so hard-to-please family members might like it. It contains vitamins A and C, iron, and some B vitamins. You can even eat the skin. Also, for the recipes that call for soy sauce, I recommend the brand San-J organic.

White Chia Miso Soup

Makes 4 servings

Hidden Treasures: seeds, miso, and tofu

This recipe offers miso soup with a twist. The tofu and chia seeds add bulk and extra nutrition while the miso adds probiotics for intestinal health. When warm comfort food is needed, this is a great meal to serve.

¼ cup chia seeds
4 cups water
2 tablespoons chickpea miso paste
2 ounces tofu
1 tablespoon green onion tops (optional)
1 tablespoon seaweed flakes (optional)

Soak the chia seeds in the water just until they soften, 10 minutes.

Put the chia seeds, water, miso paste, and tofu in a blender and process until smooth. Transfer the miso mixture into a soup pot and warm over medium-low heat for 5 to 10 minutes. Ladle the soup evenly into 4 soup bowls and sprinkle with the optional green onion and seaweed flakes. Serve immediately.

Nutritional Nugget: The most nutritious form of chia seeds is called salba. Salba is an heirloom variety and particularly high in magnesium, potassium, calcium, and iron.

Vegetable Soup

Makes 4 servings

Hidden Treasures: yam, beans, bok choy, and tomato

Vegetable soup is very soothing on a cold day especially after spending time in nature. It resembles a fall minestrone soup without the pasta. Serve with warm sprouted whole grain pita bread.

1 large yam
¼ cup cooked azuki red beans, drained and rinsed
4 bok choy leaves, torn
½ cup plus 6 cups vegetable broth
2 tomatoes, cubed
2 tablespoons Italian herbs
2 teaspoons salt (optional)

Put the yam on a cookie sheet and bake at 350 degrees F for 60 minutes or until the centers are soft. Slightly cool and peel the yam and potato and transfer them into a food processor. Add the beans, bok choy, and ½ cup of broth to the food processer. Blend into a liquid. Add the tomato and pulse-chop, leaving chunky pieces in the liquid.

Put the remaining 3 cups of vegetable broth into a pot. Add the potato mixture to the broth and cook over medium-high heat. Add the herbs, stirring occasionally until the mixture is well blended. Serve when warm.

Butternut Squash Soup

Makes 4 servings

Hidden Treasures: broth, coconut, and cashews

The sweet nature of butternut squash slightly warmed with a hint of spices and combined with the rich texture of coconut milk is sure to please. The color and texture make this soup truly a comfort food.

3 cups cooked butternut squash
1 cup vegetable broth
1 cup Coconut Magic Milk (page 35) or store-bought unsweetened coconut milk
1 teaspoon allspice
¼ cup cashews (optional)

Place the squash, broth, milk, allspice, and cashews in a blender. Mix on high until completely blended and slightly warmed. Serve immediately or transfer to a pot and heat to desired temperature.

Baked Potato-Leek Soup

Makes 4 servings

Hidden Treasures: vegetables and chickpeas

Despite its name this soup has a sophisticated taste that is just subtle enough to be a crowd pleaser. It is incredibly easy to make and can be eaten as a soup or turned into a sauce. Serve with a side of kale chips and garlic-flavored whole wheat pita wedges and enjoy a complete family meal.

2 large Yukon potatoes with peels
2 leeks, white and light green parts washed and sliced into ¼ -inch slices
1 tablespoon coconut oil
1 cup chopped yellow onion
2 garlic gloves, minced
½ cup cooked chickpeas
4 cups vegetable broth
1 teaspoon salt
¼ teaspoon Italian herbs or rosemary

Wash potatoes and leeks. Poke holes in the potatoes, put them in the oven, and cook at 350 degrees F until a fork can easily be inserted all the way through, about 45 minutes. Set potatoes aside and allow to cool.

Meanwhile, heat a 4-quart soup pot over medium heat and add the oil. Add the leek and onions and sauté for about 5 minutes, stirring often, until the onions begin to turn translucent. Add the garlic and stir well. Cook for 1 minute more. Turn off the heat and set aside.

When the potatoes are done, let them cook and then cut them into ¼-inch cubes. Transfer the leek mixture, potatoes, chickpeas, broth, salt, and herbs to a high-speed blender. Slowly turn the blender on until it reaches high speed. Blend until all the ingredients are disguised and the mixture resembles a creamy soup. Pour the soup into the pot and gently warm to desired temperature. Serve immediately.

Gina D. Diamond, M.Ed.

Cream of Mushroom Soup

Makes 4 servings

Hidden Treasures: mushroom, walnuts, red onion, and spinach

Blended mushrooms offer a rich flavor and provide a great disguise for the spinach while the walnuts and arrowroot combine for a creamy texture.

4 cups chopped mushroom, preferably portabellas
4 cups water
1 cup walnuts
½ cup chopped red onion
½ cup spinach leaves
¼ cup soy sauce
2 tablespoons arrowroot
2 teaspoons Italian seasoning

Put the mushrooms, water, walnuts, red onion, spinach, soy sauce, arrowroot, and Italian seasoning in a high-speed blender and process until smooth. Serve cold or pour the mixture into a medium soup pot and warm.

Nutritional Nugget: Arrowroot is a starch that is often used to thicken recipes. It contains iron, magnesium, and vitamin B-6. Look for it in the bulk section of your supermarket.

Casseroles and Main Dishes

A big challenge for parents, as far as food is concerned, is getting our kids to try new meals. Many children prefer plates with separated food items versus mixed together in a casserole. However, preparing meals that are new or that your family once said they did not like is useful because you never know when the tide might turn. Accompanying such meals with something that you know your family will like, such as brown rice, and putting out a platter of raw vegetables with dinner will ensure they won't go hungry. It will also round out the meal nutritionally. Family members may need to see a new entree several times before they are willing to try it, so do not give up!

Chili

Makes 6 servings

Hidden Treasure: vegetable broth and tahini

This chili has lot of flavor without being spicy. Meat lovers and vegetarians alike enjoy this chili, especially because the tahini adds a creamer texture to this already flavorful meal. Serve on a cold winter's night with a side of Corn Bread (page 82).

1 tablespoon coconut oil
1 medium-sized red onion, chopped
1 cup vegetables of choice (corn, red peppers, mushrooms, and/or cooked pumpkin wedges), diced
2 garlic cloves, minced
1 28-ounce can fire-roasted diced tomatoes
3 tablespoons tomato paste
2 tablespoons chili powder
½ cup vegetable broth
2 teaspoons salt
¼ cup tahini
1.5 cup cooked or canned black beans

Put the oil, onion, vegetables, and garlic in a small pan. Sauté over low heat until the onions are soft, about 5 minutes. Put the tomatoes, paste, powder, broth and salt in a large cooking pot and simmer over low heat for 10 minutes. Add beans, tahini, and cooked vegetable mixture to the pot. Continue cooking for 10 minutes. Serve warm.

Nutritional Nugget: Most soy grown in the United States is genetically modified so please buy organic if you add tofu to this dish.

Gina D. Diamond, M.Ed.

Mac and Cheese

Makes 4 small servings

Hidden Treasures: nuts, nutritional yeast, kelp powder, and cauliflower

This creamy mac and cheese uses almond milk, nutritional yeast, and soy as its base. The yeast can be an acquired taste, so use less than the recipe calls for as a starting point and then slowly increase the amount. Garnish the serving plates with sweet peas for some added protein.

Mac:
1 ½ pounds whole grain pasta

Nutritional Yeast Cheese Sauce:
This cheese spread can be smothered on a bagel, as well as adding texture and taste to pasta.

1 ½ cups Nut Milk (page 33) or unsweetened store-bought option
1 cup nutritional yeast
1 cup extra virgin olive oil
½ cup water
⅛ cup soy sauce
1 ½ cups cauliflower, chopped
3-ounce block organic firm (not silken) tofu
1 teaspoon kelp powder or salt
1 teaspoon garlic powder (optional)
1 tablespoon paprika (optional)
1 dollop mustard (optional)

Cook the pasta according to the directions.
   Put the milk, yeast, oil, water, soy sauce, cauliflower, tofu, kelp, garlic powder, paprika, and mustard into a blender and process until smooth. Pour the mixture into a baking pan and add the pasta. Bake for 35 minutes at 300 degrees F.

Nutritional Nuggets: Nutritional yeast is a source of vitamin B-12, rich in folic and amino acids, and contains iron. Also, kelp powder can be used in place of salt. It contains iodine and trace minerals that are lacking in the soil but found in the sea.

Vegetable-Rice Pie

Makes 8 servings

Hidden Treasures: lentils, red pepper, carrots, and herbs

It can be a challenge to find store-bought vegetarian entrees and even harder to find options that contain nutrient-dense ingredients. This homemade option is so much better, and as a bonus, the magnesium found in the lentils will help the calcium in the kale become more bioavailable. Serve with spaghetti squash sprinkled with olive oil, salt, nutritional yeast, and a handful of Green Chips (page 84). Top with Powerful Pink Sauce (page 50). This recipe can be time intensive but in the end, quite exotic and worth the trouble.

1 cup cooked lentils
2 tablespoons ground flaxseeds
6 tablespoons water
½ cup rolled oats
1 garlic clove
½ red pepper, chopped
1 large carrot, chopped
1 cup cooked brown rice
2 tablespoons Italian seasoning
3 tablespoons soy sauce
1 tablespoon onion powder
1 tablespoon freshly squeezed lemon juice

Put the drained lentils into a medium bowl and mash them into a paste. While the paste is cooling, put the flaxseeds and water into a bowl, stirring occasionally, until a gel forms.

Finely chop the oats, garlic, pepper, and carrot in a food processor. Transfer this mixture into the lentil bowl and add the flax gel, rice, seasoning, soy sauce, onion powder, and lemon juice. Mix by hand until all the ingredients are blended.

Pour the pie contents evenly into a 9-inch pie pan that has been lightly coated with raw coconut oil. Place the pan in the oven, turn the temperature to 350 degrees F, and bake for 20 minutes. Top with Powerful Pink Sauce (page 50) or your favorite marinara sauce and bake for an additional 10 minutes. This pie can be stored in the refrigerator for 1 week when covered.

Gina D. Diamond, M.Ed.

Nutritional Nugget: The nutrients in seeds, nuts, and beans become more available to the human body when they are soaked in water and sprouted. This can easily be done at home with a bit of lead time, but it is best to purchase flaxseeds that are sprouted and purchased from a company you trust.

Lively Latkes

Makes 4 servings

Hidden Treasures: cauliflower, sweet potato, celery, and seeds

Latkes (potato pancakes) are traditionally eaten during the Jewish holiday, Chanukah. They taste great but don't offer much in the way of nutrition. With a few small variations, you can still enjoy this meal and give your body more of what it needs. Top with Applesauce (page 48) and serve with a side salad. Enjoy all year long.

2 tablespoons ground flaxseed
6 tablespoons water
1 cup cauliflower florets
1 cup chopped celery
½ yellow onion
2 large potatoes, peeled
1 sweet potato, peeled
¼ cup sodium-free matzo meal or whole grain breadcrumbs
½ teaspoon sea salt (optional)
½ teaspoon pepper (optional)

Soak the flaxseeds in water until a gel forms, stirring occasionally.

Put the cauliflower, celery, and onion in a food processor and finely chop.

Grate the potatoes and put them into a mixing bowl. Add the finely chopped vegetables, flax mixture, breadcrumbs, salt, and pepper. Mix the ingredients together. Form into pancakes by taking a spoonful into your hand, rolling into a ball, and flattening with your palm. Place on a baking sheet that has been lightly coated with raw coconut oil and cook for 25 minutes at 250 degrees F. Turn the pancakes over and bake for another 10 minutes or until golden crispy. Serve warm.

Tasty Gems: Remember to oil pots, pans, and muffin tins with raw coconut oil instead of olive oil. Coconut oil is less susceptible to chemical damage when heated. Also, Mary's Gone Crackers just came out with a breadcrumb alternative that is organic and gluten-free.

Gina D. Diamond, M.Ed.

Pizza

Makes 4 servings

Hidden Treasures: rice, soy, cauliflower, and herbs

This pizza is really fun to make as each family member can participate. Even young children can help make the dough and select their own toppings. Simply put out a salad bar with lots of topping options such as chopped pineapple, mushrooms, tomatoes, and butternut squash. You can even offer raw kale and broccoli brushed with olive oil and sea salt.

Crust
1 ½ cups cooked brown rice
1 ½ cups cooked or canned soybeans
¼ cup extra-virgin olive oil
½ cup diced cauliflower
2 teaspoons Italian seasoning
½ teaspoon sea salt

Put the rice, beans, oil, cauliflower, seasoning, and salt in a food processor and combine until the mixture starts to ball up. Spread the mixture to desired thickness onto a baking tray that has been lightly coated with coconut oil. Top with Raw Red Marinara Sauce (page 51) and Nutritional Yeast Cheese Spread (see page 70). Place the tray in the oven, turn the heat to 250 degrees F, and bake for 45 minutes or until the crust is golden brown. Serve when warm.

Nutritional Nugget: Daiya cheese is often the preferred choice for who do not consume dairy. While it is quite tasty, Daiya is a processed product that is not made from organic ingredients. Encourage your family to try a pizza without dairy or purchase cheese from a small family farm under the Organic Valley umbrella.

Quinoa Bowl

Makes 4 servings

Hidden Treasure: seeds

This recipe is super simple to make. Quinoa is healthful and hearty so it can pass as a meal, especially if it is accompanied by edamame and a salad.

1 cup quinoa
2 cups water
2 tablespoons hemp seeds or ground flaxseeds

Put rinsed quinoa and the water into a pan with a lid. Slowly bring to a boil and simmer on a low heat until the water is totally absorbed by the grains, about 15 minutes. Let the quinoa cool slightly and mix in the hemp seeds. Serve immediately.

Nutritional Nugget: Quinoa is a seed that can be prepared like a grain. It is a complete protein and contains manganese, magnesium, and iron.

Shepherd's Pie

Makes 4 servings

Hidden Treasures: onion, mushrooms, tomato, zucchini, and walnuts

Enjoy this hearty meal in the winter months and top with leftover Mouth-Watering Mashed Potatoes (page 81) to enhance the nutritional value of this dish. The longer it sits, the thicker it gets, so consider making it the night before you plan to eat it.

2 cups vegetable broth
½ small red onion, chopped
4 white mushrooms, chopped
1 large chopped tomato
½ small zucchini, chopped
⅛ cup ground walnuts
2 tablespoons tomato paste
2 tablespoons organic soy sauce
1 tablespoon Italian seasoning
2 tablespoons cornstarch
4 tablespoons water
1 large carrot, chopped
½ cup green peas
4 cups Mouth-Watering Mashed Potatoes (page 81)

Put the broth, red onion, mushrooms, tomato, zucchini, walnuts, tomato paste, soy sauce, and seasoning into a high-speed blender and process until smooth. Pour the stock mixture into a soup pot, over medium-low heat. In a separate bowl, dissolve the cornstarch in the water and add it to the stock. Simmer to thicken, about 2 minutes.

   Pour the stock into a 2 ½ quart casserole dish. Add the carrot and peas. Spread the Mouth-Watering Mashed Potatoes over the top and cook for 1 hour at 250 degrees F. Serve warm.

Tostadas

Makes 4 servings

Hidden Treasures: amaranth and red pepper

Many people enjoy Mexican food. Now you can make some at home with organic whole ingredients that taste great when topped with beans, salsa, and Guacamole (page 55). Another great recipe offered to me from Cherie Calbom.

2 cups amaranth flour or whole-wheat flour
1 teaspoon salt
4 tablespoons coconut oil
½ cup warm water
¼ cup finely shredded red pepper
¼ cup corn kernels

Put the flour, salt, oil, water, pepper, and corn in a medium bowl and mix, forming the dough. Cut the dough into 4 equal parts and roll each into a ball. Using your hand or a rolling pin, flatten the balls into tortillas, using more flour if needed.

Put each tortilla into a pan, lightly coated with coconut oil cooking on both sides, until they are dry and resemble a crisp tostada. Repeat until all the tostadas are cooked. When cooled, put them into a reused plastic bag and place in the refrigerator for 1 week or freeze for later use.

Nutritional Nugget: Amaranth is a seed that is used as a grain. It is a great source of essential amino acids, calcium, iron, magnesium, and vitamins C, B and K.

Corn Tortillas

Makes 16–20 tortillas

Hidden Treasure: psyllium

These tortillas are a great example of how raw food can be easy to prepare and pleasing to the taste buds. You can eat these the traditional way or turn them into a pizza by topping them with nut cheese and raw tomato sauce.

5 corn ears
2 tablespoons psyllium husk powder (not seed)
Purified water as needed

Cut the corn kernels off the cob and place them in a food processor with the psyllium powder. Blend until smooth, adding water as needed. The batter should be the consistency of pancake batter. Place large spoonfuls of the batter on dehydrator Paraflex sheets. Using a spoon, swirl the batter in a circular motion to shape into rounds to your desired tortilla size. Dehydrate the batter for 4 hours at 105 degrees F. Flip the tortillas and dehydrate for another 2 hours or until the tortillas are no longer wet yet soft and easy to roll. You can also make this recipe in the oven if you don't have a dehydrator.

Nutritional Nugget: Psyllium powder is derived from gel-coated seeds and is a natural thickener. It aids in digestion and helps to regulate cholesterol and blood glucose levels.

Side Dishes

Side dishes are wonderful to serve because they are very versatile. They taste great on their own, or you can serve several sides as a meal or combine with a snack for a hearty option. Enjoy what works for you and your family.

Mashed Potatoes

Makes 4 servings

Hidden Treasures: coconut milk, cauliflower, and seeds

This recipe is easy to make and the taste is rich and creamy. It can be eaten as a side dish or made to top a main meal such as Shepherd's Pie (page 76).

3 medium Yukon potatoes
1 cup Coconut Magic Milk (page 35) or store-bought unsweetened coconut milk
½ cup shredded cauliflower
1 tablespoon sesame seeds
½ teaspoon brown rice miso or garbanzo miso, or salt (optional)

Cook the potatoes for 1 hour at 350 degrees F. Let them cool slightly and then peel and discard the skins. Mash the potatoes in a wide bowl until smooth. Add the milk, cauliflower, seeds, and miso; mix until fully blended. Eat while warm.

Nutritional Nuggets: Potato skins can be left on if you have more adventurous eaters as the skins increase the nutritional value of the dish because they contain vitamins and fiber. Also, miso is a fermented paste usually made from soy. I prefer to purchase the rice or garbanzo varieties. Miso contains B vitamins, essential amino acids, and probiotics to restore intestinal health.

Gina D. Diamond, M.Ed.

Corn Bread

Makes 6 servings

Hidden Treasures: quinoa and red peppers

This subtly sweet corn bread is great by itself, smothered in olive oil and honey, or crumbled over Chili (page 69). It is best served warm.

1 cup cornmeal
1 cup coconut milk
1 cup whole-wheat flour
1 teaspoon baking powder
1 teaspoon baking soda
½ teaspoon salt (optional)
1 cup cooked quinoa
¼ cup melted coconut oil
1 large egg
¼ cup maple syrup
¼ cup diced red peppers

Combine the cornmeal and milk in a small bowl. Stir and then set aside until the cornmeal has soaked up the water, about 5 minutes.

Mix the flour, baking powder, baking soda, and salt in a 10 inch greased iron skillet or other baking dish. Add the cooked quinoa and stir with a wooden spoon. In another bowl, mix the egg, oil, and maple syrup until a paste forms and then pour it into the flour mixture. Stir the batter again. Add the cornmeal and milk mixture and continue to stir until all the ingredients are fully integrated. Add the peppers and gently fold into the mixture. Put the skillet in the oven and bake for 35 minutes at 350 degrees F.

Nutritional Nugget: Raw olive oil is the best as it is unrefined, unheated, and unprocessed. If raw is unavailable, select cold-pressed extra virgin olive oil.

Variation: If you want a buttermilk flavor, whisk the milk with 2 teaspoons of freshly squeezed lemon juice. Let the liquid sit for 5 minutes and then continue following the recipe.

Squashbrowns

Makes 4 servings

Hidden Treasures: squash and nutritional yeast

These are a nice twist to the traditional potato hash browns with a long list of vitamins and minerals to boot. Serve with Applesauce (page 48) for a small meal or as a side to pancakes or Fabulous French Toast (page 27). Either way, they are best served warm.

4 cups spaghetti squash, roasted
¼ yellow onion, chopped and sautéed (optional)
1 teaspoon coconut oil
4 teaspoons nutritional yeast
Butter spread (optional)
Salt and pepper, to taste

Remove the moisture from the squash using a potato ricer or paper towels. Place the squash in a bowl and mix in sautéed onion.

Lightly coat a skillet with coconut oil and turn the heat to medium. Put one large mound of the squash in the pan and cook until slightly brown, about 5 minutes. Flip the mound occasional and cook for an additional 5 minutes. Remove the squashbrowns and place them on a tray. Lather with coconut oil butter spread made by Earth Balance and sprinkle with nutritional yeast, salt, and pepper if so desired. Serve immediately.

Nutritional Nuggets: Nutritional yeast is a source of vitamin B-12, rich in folic and amino acids, and contains iron. Spaghetti squash has modest amounts of vitamins A and C, fiber, and calcium.

Green Chips

Makes 4 servings

Hidden Treasures: leafy greens and nutritional yeast

You will be amazed at how good these chips taste. Kids who do not normally eat kale will love them. This recipe can help anyone kick the traditional chip habit and get a wonderful boost of nutrients to boot.

1 large bunch leafy greens (kale, lettuce, beet tops, spinach, and so forth)
2 tablespoons melted coconut oil
1 teaspoon sea salt
1 tablespoon nutritional yeast (optional)

Clip the stems off and put the leaves into a medium bowl. Mix the leaves in the olive oil until they are well coated. Spread them out on 2 baking sheets and place the sheets in the oven. Turn the oven to 250 degrees F and bake them for 25 minutes. Remove the leaves from the sheets and put them in a medium bowl. Sprinkle them with the salt and nutritional yeast, and place in a sealed container. The chips will last for 1 month but are best eaten fresh out of the oven.

Nutritional Nugget: Nutritional yeast has a cheesy flavor and is a source of B-12, folic and amino acids, and iron.

Raw Variation: Put the oil-drizzled leaves on dehydrator sheets and dry them at 105 degrees F for 2 hours.

Veggie Home Fries

Makes 4 servings

Hidden Treasures: parsnip, eggplant, and nutritional yeast

Enjoy these home fries as a snack or as a side to any burger recipe in this book. When they become slightly browned, the parsnip and eggplant begin to look very similar to the potato cubes.

3 medium Yukon potatoes, cubed
1 small parsnip, peeled and cubed
1 cup eggplant, peeled and cubed
sea salt and nutritional yeast, to taste (optional)

Liberally coat a skillet with coconut oil. Put the potato and parsnip pieces in a skillet and cook on medium heat for 5 minutes, stirring occasionally. Add more oil as needed. Turn the heat down to medium-low and cook for 10 more minutes, continuing to stir. Add the eggplant and cook for an additional 5 minutes. Put the home fries in a bowl and season with salt and yeast, to taste.

Tasty Gem: The potato, parsnip, and eggplant cubes should be roughly the same size for a better-disguised effect.

Snacks and Treats

Aside from desserts, children tend to like snack food more than any other, so it makes sense to prepare delicious and healthful snacks to have ready when your family members get hungry. Simply prepare the food ahead of time and put a few options in small bowls when they are ready to eat. You can keep it simple by offering seeds, carrots, and a green smoothie, or you can offer up one or more of the following recipes. When preparing a snack that requires baking or a considerable amount of time to prepare, double or triple the recipe and freeze some for later use. These snacks are great to take on outings, too.

You will be doing some baking in this section. I typically do not preheat my oven because it is a more environmentally conscious choice as this practice uses less energy. My recipes are written in this way and the baking times designated account for this practice.

Fruit Leathers

The snack section begins with fruit leathers because almost every kid that has tried them loves them. They are a nice alternative to the ones you find in the store because they are fresher, use less packaging, come in more creative flavors, and offer more than just fruit. Even though they are a healthful choice for the body they are not so great for the teeth. Because they are sticky and hang around in crevices, offer your child a raw carrot after consuming fruit leathers. The carrot acts as a natural toothbrush and provides a reason to eat another vegetable.

Fruit leathers are best made in a dehydrator because you can dry them at a very low temperature, which keeps their nutrients intact. For that reason, I recommend that your next kitchen purchase is a dehydrator (see Making Conscious Eating Choices). Practice using the dehydrator to make leathers. Once you begin feeling more confident, you can expand by trying some of my other raw recipes.

If you do not own a dehydrator and you are ready to get started, I recommend that you borrow one or cook the leathers in an oven at 170 degrees F (or lowest temperature on oven) for 12–15 hours. Simply put unbleached parchment paper on several cookie sheets and coat with coconut oil. Pour the fruit mixture onto the sheets (about 4 cups per sheet) and spread the liquid evenly until the paper is covered. Half-way through brush with water. The leathers are ready when they are no longer sticky and peel off the paper with ease.

Strawberry-Banana Leathers

Makes 32 servings

Hidden Treasures: beet greens and strawberry hulls

Bananas and strawberries make a wonderful combination and do their due diligence to hide the beet leaves. Spin them all together, dehydrate and viola — you have one healthful snack.

2 pounds strawberries, sliced with hulls intact
2 large bananas, sliced
2 large apples, chopped
4–8 green beet leaves, to taste
¼ cup water (optional)

Put the strawberries, bananas, apples, beet leaves, and water into a high-speed blender and process until smooth. Stop occasionally to scrape the sides of the blender while moving the mixture towards the blades if needed. Taste and add more greens if the mixture is very sweet.

Put four ¼ cup mounds of mixture on each dehydrator sheet and spread with a spoon until the mixture is thinned but the sheet is not visible. Dehydrate at 105 degrees F for approximately 8 hours. Check the leathers after 7 hours, removing them as soon as they are ready. Scrape them off easily by using the flat edge of a knife or a clean fingernail. Roll the leathers individually into a cigar shape. Place in a tightly covered container and store at room temperature. Leathers will last 1 month.

Nutritional Nugget: Strawberry hulls (green stems) are filled with minerals and chlorophyll, which is known to cleanse the body, fight infection, heal wounds, and promote the health of the circulatory, digestive, immune, and detoxification systems.

Breathtaking Blueberry-Banana Leathers

Makes 32 servings

Hidden Treasure: broccoli

It is tough to get kids to eat raw broccoli and that is why it works so well to hide some in smoothies or fruit leathers. The broccoli is totally undetectable until you are ready to share your surprise because of the color of the blueberries and the sweetness of the fruit.

8 cups blueberries
2 large bananas
½ apple, cut into pieces
2 cups broccoli florets
¼ cup water (optional)

Put the blueberries, bananas, apples, broccoli, and water into a high-speed blender and process until smooth. Stop occasionally to scrape the sides of the blender while moving the mixture towards the blades if needed.

Put four ¼ cup mounds of mixture on each dehydrator sheet and spread with a spoon until the mixture is thinned but the sheet is not visible. Dehydrate at 105 degrees F for approximately 8 hours. Check the leathers after 7 hours, removing them as soon as they are ready. Scrape them off easily by using the flat edge of a knife or a clean fingernail. Roll the leathers individually into a cigar shape. Place in a tightly covered container and store at room temperature. Leathers will last one month.

Mango Leathers

Makes 32 servings

Hidden Treasures: bell pepper and bok choy

The secret to this recipe is getting ripe sweet mangoes that easily hide the taste of the hidden treasures. Enjoy with a swirl of Barlean's berry omega oil for a refreshing tropical fruit taste.

9 mangoes, sliced
1 ½ orange bell peppers, chopped
¾ cup bok choy, white stalks only
8 teaspoons berry omega oil (optional)

Put the mangoes, bell peppers, and bok choy into a high-speed blender and process until smooth. Stop occasionally to scrape the sides of the blender while moving the mixture towards the blades if needed. Taste and add more vegetables if the mixture is very sweet.

Put four ¼ cup mounds of mixture on each dehydrator sheet and spread with a spoon until the mixture is thinned but the sheet is not visible. Drop ¼ teaspoon of omega oil on each leather. Dehydrate at 105 degrees F for approximately 8 hours. Check the leathers after 7 hours, removing them as soon as they are ready. Scrape them off easily by using the flat edge of a knife or a clean fingernail. Roll the leathers individually into a cigar shape. Place in a tightly covered container and store at room temperature. Leathers will last one month.

Nutritional Nugget: Choose a raw, vegan, and organic Omega 3-6-9 liquid from a company that you trust.

Pineapple-Strawberry Leathers

Makes 32 servings

Hidden Treasures: jicama and seeds

If you are in need of a delicious and refreshing recipe for fruit leathers, then this one is for you. The pineapple gives it a tropical flavor while the strawberries offer a beautiful hue.

9 cups pineapple, chopped
24 large strawberries, halved with hull intact
3 cups jicama, peeled and chopped
1½ apples, chopped
3 teaspoons hemp seeds or sunflower seeds

Put the pineapple, strawberries, jicama, apples, and hemp seeds into a high-speed blender and process until smooth. Stop occasionally to scrape the sides of the blender while moving the mixture towards the blades if needed. Taste and add more greens if the mixture is very sweet.

Put four ¼ cup mounds of mixture on each dehydrator sheet and spread with a spoon until the mixture is thinned but the sheet is not visible. Dehydrate at 105 degrees F for approximately 8 hours. Check the leathers after 7 hours, removing them as soon as they are ready. Scrape them off easily by using the flat edge of a knife or a clean fingernail. Roll the leathers individually into a cigar shape. Place in a tightly covered container and store at room temperature. Leathers will last one month.

Nutritional Nuggets: Strawberry hulls give added nutrition, jicama is a great source of vitamin C, and hemp seeds are a complete protein and contain essential fats.

Gina D. Diamond, M.Ed.

Kiwi-Pineapple-Mango Leathers

Makes 32 servings

Hidden Treasures: lettuce and seeds

This recipe has a lovely tropical flavor and the kiwis hide the hidden treasures well. The leathers taste best if the fruit is slightly ripe.

8 kiwis
2 pineapples
4 mangos
2 romaine lettuce heads
1 cup water
1 cup coconut butter
¼ cup hemp seeds or sunflower seeds

Put the kiwis, pineapple, mangos, lettuce, water, butter, and hemp seeds into a high-speed blender and process until smooth. Stop occasionally to scrape the sides of the blender while moving the mixture towards the blades if needed. Taste and add more greens if the mixture is very sweet.

Put four ¼ cup mounds of mixture on each dehydrator sheet and spread with a spoon until the mixture is thinned but the sheet is not visible. Dehydrate at 105 degrees F for approximately 8 hours. Check the leathers after 7 hours, removing them as soon as they are ready. Scrape them off easily by using the flat edge of a knife or a clean fingernail. Roll the leathers individually into a cigar shape. Place in a tightly covered container and store at room temperature. Leathers will last one month.

Tasty Gem: Consider soaking seeds, nuts, oats, and legumes in water before you use them in recipes. This will aid in digestion.

Plum Leathers

Makes 32 servings

Hidden Treasures: beets, chard, and seeds

The dark color of a plum's skin is a great mask for most hidden treasures, and because chard has a subtle taste, the two ingredients work well together. Adding a few poppy seeds will slightly increase the nutrient value because they contain fatty acids and essential oils, vitamin B, and a number of minerals.

16 red ripe plums (Brooks are particularly good for dehydrating)
4 large sweet apples
1 ⅓ cup water
¼ cup red beets, chopped
3 chard leaves
1 teaspoon poppy seeds

Put the plums, apples, water, beets, chard, and seeds into a high-speed blender and process until smooth. Stop occasionally to scrape the sides of the blender while moving the mixture towards the blades if needed. Taste and add more apple if the mixture is too tart.

Put four ¼ cup mounds of mixture on each dehydrator sheet and spread with a spoon until the mixture is thinned but the sheet is not visible. Dehydrate at 105 degrees F for approximately 8 hours. Check the leathers after 7 hours, removing them as soon as they are ready. Scrape them off easily by using the flat edge of a knife or a clean fingernail. Roll the leathers individually into a cigar shape. Place in a tightly covered container and store at room temperature. Leathers will last one month.

Nutritional Nugget: Poppy seeds are high in magnesium, making it easier for your body to absorb the calcium these seeds provide.

Gina D. Diamond, M.Ed.

Nectarine Leathers

Makes 32 servings

Hidden Treasures: seeds, miner's lettuce, and carrots

Nectarines are best when they are in season and can be bought directly from a local farm. Their beautiful color nicely camouflages the hidden treasures, so consider adding more vegetables as your family becomes accustomed to their taste.

25 ripe nectarines, chopped
5 tablespoons ground flaxseed
2 ½ cups miner's lettuce, loosely packed
2 large carrots, chopped
¼ cup water (optional)

Put the nectarines, flaxseeds, miner's lettuce, carrots, and water into a high-speed blender and process until smooth. Stop occasionally to scrape the sides of the blender while moving the mixture towards the blades if needed. Taste and add more greens if the mixture is very sweet.

Put four ¼ cup mounds of mixture on each dehydrator sheet and spread with a spoon until the mixture is thinned but the sheet is not visible. Dehydrate at 105 degrees F for approximately 8 hours. Check the leathers after 7 hours, removing them as soon as they are ready. Scrape them off easily by using the flat edge of a knife or a clean fingernail. Roll the leathers individually into a cigar shape. Place in a tightly covered container and store at room temperature. Leathers will last one month.

Nutritional Nugget: Miner's lettuce is a vine that usually grows wild. It is best to grow it in a contained area or purchase it at a farmer's market. Miner's lettuce is high in vitamin C, beta carotene, and protein.

Variation: Replace 2 ½ cups of miner's lettuce with 2 ½ cups of spinach.

Almond-Banana-Date Leathers

Makes 32 leathers

Hidden Treasures: almonds, eggplant, and cauliflower

Kids are so wild about the taste of bananas and dates that they are often surprised to learn that they are consuming a healthful dose of almonds and cauliflower. Do not be surprised if this fruit leather becomes a favorite in your household.

6 cups Nut Milk (page 33) or unsweetened store-bought option
¾ cup chopped eggplant
3 large bananas
15 small pitted dates, soaked
1 ½ cup chopped cauliflower

Put the almond milk, eggplant, banana, dates, and cauliflower into a high-speed blender and process until smooth. Stop occasionally to scrape the sides of the blender while moving the mixture towards the blades if needed. Taste and add more greens if the mixture is very sweet.

Put four ¼ cup mounds of mixture on each dehydrator sheet and spread with a spoon until the mixture is thinned but the sheet is not visible. Dehydrate at 105 degrees F for approximately 8 hours. Check the leathers after 7 hours, removing them as soon as they are ready. Scrape them off easily by using the flat edge of a knife or a clean fingernail. Roll the leathers individually into a cigar shape. Place in an airtight container and store at room temperature. Leathers will last one month.

Nutritional Nugget: Medjool dates are the healthiest natural sweetener. You can use them in some recipes instead of sugar.

Vegetable Crackers

Makes 12 servings

Hidden Treasures: seeds, celery, almonds, carrot, and kelp

Crackers make a wonderful snack, and these are a gluten-free option packed with protein, vitamins, and minerals. They go great with any type of spread including Extra-Green Guacamole (page 55), Cashew Cream Cheese Spread (page 53), or Perky Pesto (page 47).

1 ½ cups ground flaxseeds
½ cup chopped celery
½ cup chopped tomato
½ cup almonds
½ cup sunflower seeds
¼ cup chopped carrot
1 teaspoon kelp powder (optional)
Sea salt, to taste

In a food processor, blend the flaxseeds, celery, tomato, almonds, sunflower seeds, carrot, and kelp powder. Taste and add desired amount of sea salt. Transfer dough to a wood block and roll with a lightly floured rolling pin to get as thin as possible.

Lightly oil a baking tray with coconut oil. Spread the cracker mixture on the tray. Score the mixture with a knife to mark the cracker size before baking. Bake for 30 minutes at 300 degrees F. Remove from the oven and let cool.

Nutritional Nugget: Kelp is a salty sea vegetable and its powder form is a healthful alternative to salt as it contains iodine, iron, and antioxidants.

Tasty Gem: Seeds high in essential fatty acids such as flaxseeds should not be heated above 300 degrees F as the healthful oil will turn into an unhealthful fat at a higher temperature.

Strawberry-Oat Bars

Makes 16 servings

Hidden Treasures: red pepper, seeds, and maca powder

These bars do not contain cane sugar yet they are sweet and filling. Enjoy them for breakfast or offer them up after your child's big game.

2 cups oats
½ cup sunflower seeds
2 teaspoons hemp seeds (optional)
16 large pitted dates, soaked in water for about 2 hours or until soft
½ cup red pepper, chopped
2 teaspoons maca powder (optional)
2 large strawberries, sliced and dehulled

Combine 1 cup of the oats and all the seeds in a food processor and grind until the consistency of flour. Add the dates, red pepper, and maca to the flour and mix until you achieve a dough-like texture. Put the oat mixture in a medium bowl and stir in the strawberries and the remaining cup of oats by hand. Shape the mixture into thin squares and place on baking sheets. Bake at 250 degrees F for 25 minutes.

Nutritional Nugget: Maca, an herb from the Andes dubbed as a superfood, can be found in the bulk section of your health food store. It is known to support the immune system and increase energy. It is a strong herb so it is best to check with a trusted medical professional to ask about serving maca to your child(ren).

Raw Variation: Dehydrate the bars at 105 degrees F for 10 hours. For a crispier bar, flip halfway through and dehydrate for 2 more hours.

Crazy Cantaloupe Candies

Makes 32 servings

Hidden Treasure: cantaloupe

You may be thinking that candy belongs in the desert section. You can certainly eat these candy pieces as dessert but because they contain only fruit, they make a healthful snack. Do be mindful of how well-dried fruit sticks to teeth, and ask your child to eat a carrot after consuming their Crazy Cantaloupe Candies.

1 large cantaloupe, thinly sliced

Put the cantaloupe pieces on a dehydrator sheet and cook at 110 degrees F for 8 hours. Flip the pieces halfway through. Remove the pieces when they are completely dry on both sides. Place in airtight container and store at room temperature. The cantaloupe pieces will last for 1 month.

Botanical Raspberry-Orange Biscuits

Makes 25 servings

Hidden Treasures: zucchini, beet, walnuts, and seeds

Even beet haters will eat these bars because they taste so darn good. They make a great party snack around Christmastime because of their beautiful red color or offer them as a fun treat on "eat a rainbow" day.

2 cups grated zucchini
1 medium red beet, grated
2 cups grated apples
1 cup walnuts
1 cup almonds
1 cup raspberries
1 cup dried apples, chopped
1 cup ground flaxseeds
1 ½ cups fresh-squeezed orange juice (3 oranges)
2 cups rolled oats
2–4 tablespoons maple syrup or coconut nectar (optional)

Mix the zucchini, beets, and fresh apples in a medium mixing bowl and set aside.
Chop the nuts using a food processor until pulverized. Transfer to the zucchini bowl and add the berries, dried apples, and seeds, stirring just to coat. Add the orange juice and oats and continue stirring for 1 minute. Taste the batter for sweetness, adding the nectar if necessary. Form the batter into biscuits using a large spoon. Cook for 25 minutes at 250 degrees F.

Raw Option: Place the batter on dehydrator sheets and dry for 5 hours at 105 degrees F. Flip and dehydrate for 4 more hours (or longer if a drier biscuit is desired). Store in an airtight container. The biscuits will last up to 1 month.

Tasty Gem: Look for the word "sundried" when choosing fruit that was dried at a low temperature. For an even more wholesome option, make sure that it was not sprayed with sulfur dioxide. Sulfur dioxide is used to enhance the color of the fruit and can easily be avoided by purchasing an organically grown option or by drying your own (see Cantaloupe Candies on page 100).

Gina D. Diamond, M.Ed.

Almond-Fig Squares

Makes 20 servings

Hidden Treasures: Brazil nuts, seeds, and cauliflower

Almonds and figs go great together and they are packed full of essential vitamins and minerals. Even kids who do not normally eat almonds and figs will enjoy this tasty snack because it is sweetened with dates and bananas.

1 ½ cups almonds
½ cup Brazil nuts
½ cup flaxseeds
½ cup cauliflower, chopped
½ tablespoon grated orange zest
2 tablespoons tahini
½ cup dates, chopped
¼ cup figs, soaked
1 ripe banana, mashed

Put the almonds, Brazil nuts, flaxseeds, and cauliflower in a blender. Process until an almond meal is formed. Scoop the meal out of the blender and put it into a medium bowl. Add the zest, tahini, dates, figs, and banana. Mix with a wooden spoon until well blended.

Take a small amount of the dough in your hand and shape into a square. Place the squares on a baking sheet and put in the refrigerator. Serve when the squares become firm, about 1 hour. Store the remaining squares in a container in the refrigerator. The squares will last 1 month.

Raw Variation: For a crunchier texture, place your squares in the dehydrator and dry them for 5 hours at 110 degrees F. Flip once halfway through.

Cinnamon-Apple Bars

Makes 20 servings

Hidden Treasures: jicama, buckwheat groats, and seeds

This recipe makes sweet bars that are a great snack during or after a sporting event. Wrap them up in unbleached parchment paper to have on the go or serve them with almonds for an after-dinner treat.

1 cup buckwheat groats, soaked
8 small pitted dates
1 cup jicama, chopped
⅛ cup hemp seeds
⅛ cup ground flaxseeds
3 medium sweet apples, chopped
½ cup raisins
3 teaspoons ground cinnamon
¼ cup maple syrup or coconut nectar (optional)

Grind the groats, dates, jicama, and seeds in a food processor into a flour consistency. Add the apples and pulse for 30 seconds. Transfer the groat mixture to a medium bowl and add the raisins, cinnamon, and nectar. Stir until blended.

Form the sticky mixture into squares and place them on 2 lightly oiled cookie sheets. Bake for 40–45 minutes at 350 degrees F, flipping halfway through. Store them in an airtight container. The bars will last 1 month.

Nutritional Nugget: Buckwheat groats are high in iron, protein, fiber, vitamins, alpha linoleic acid, and essential fatty acids. You get a lot of bang for your buck with these nuggets, and many kids will eat them because they have a nutty flavor.

Raw Variation: Place the bars on dehydrator sheets and dry at 110 degrees F for 4 hours. Flip and dehydrate for 3 more hours (or longer if a drier bar is desired).

Fruit Popsicles:

Banana Peach Popsicles

Makes 10 servings

Hidden Treasures: nuts and peppers

There is nothing like a Popsicle on a hot summer's day. Making your own are far better than anything you can find in the store. Replace the store-bought variety with a fruit-sweetened whole-food option that contains a few hidden treasures.

1 ½ cups Nut Milk (page 33) or unsweetened store-bought option
1 large banana
1 sweet peach
½ cup chopped red pepper

Combine the milk, banana, peach, and red pepper in a high-speed blender; process until smooth and creamy. Pour the mixture evenly into a Popsicle holder and insert a reusable stick in each mold. Put the holders in the freezer and mix the liquid every 5–10 minutes until it is slightly frozen. Once it has reached this point keep in the freezer for 5–10 more minutes to fully harden. Eat when ready.

Pina Colada Popsicles

Makes 8 Popsicles

Hidden Treasures: celery and seeds

These Popsicles taste best if you use a ripe pineapple. Be sure to ask the produce person at your grocery store to help you pick out the perfect pineapple that is sure to be sweet.

2 cups pineapple, chopped
½ cup Coconut Magic Milk (page 35) or store-bought unsweetened coconut milk
¾ cup celery, chopped
3 teaspoons hemp seeds
½ cup shredded coconut

Combine the pineapple, milk, celery, and seeds in a high-speed blender; process until smooth and creamy. Add the coconut and mix at a slow speed for 10 seconds. Pour the mixture evenly into a Popsicle holder and insert a reusable stick into each mold. Put in the freezer and eat when the Popsicles are frozen solid.

Nutritional Nugget: Hemp seeds are a complete protein and a great source of essential fats.

Variation: Replace 3 teaspoons of hemp seeds with 3 teaspoons of sunflower seeds.

Gina D. Diamond, M.Ed.

Limeade Popsicles

Makes 8 servings

Hidden Treasures: limes and spinach

These Popsicles have a beautiful green hue so it is easy to hide the spinach leaves. Explain to your kids that the green color is mostly due to the lime juice and that the Popsicles taste just like sweet limeade. If you get any takers, I bet they will be hooked.

½ cup lime juice (about 4 limes)
2 large sweet apples, chopped
½ ripe peach, chopped
5 spinach leaves

Juice the limes using your orange juice maker.
   Put the lime juice, apples, peach, and spinach into a blender and mix well. Pour the limeade evenly into a Popsicle holder and insert a reusable stick into each mold. Put the holder into the freezer and stir the mixture a couple of times during the freezing process to prevent the spinach from sinking to the bottom. Serve when frozen solid.

Banana Quinoa Popsicles

Makes 10 servings

Hidden Treasures: quinoa and seeds

These Popsicles remind me of a cold version of rice pudding. They are sweet, refreshing, and melt quickly, so serve them immediately after they come out of the freezer.

¼ cup cooked quinoa
7 ripe bananas, sliced
1 ½ teaspoons hemp seeds (optional)

Using a fork, mash the bananas in a medium bowl. Add the cooled quinoa and hemp seeds and continuing mashing. Spoon the mixture evenly into Popsicle holders. Insert a stick into each holder, set the holders in the freezer and eat when frozen solid.

Nutritional Nugget: Hemp seeds are a great source of complete protein and essential fats.

Desserts

And we finally made it to the dessert section. I can already hear my family cheering. Although dessert is enjoyed by most, many of us in the Western Hemisphere eat too much sugar. Reserve true desserts for special occasions such as birthdays and holidays, and turn some of the sweeter recipes in this book such as fruit leathers and Popsicles into a treat if your family is struggling with reducing their sugar intake. Use dates and bananas as a sweetener and choose coconut crystals/nectar, molasses, or maple syrup when fruit alone will not do the trick. Help your children increase their body awareness by asking them how they feel after eating certain foods, especially those containing sugar. For family members who need to get off sugar altogether, consider consuming a form of fenugreek seeds to curb the cravings.

You will notice that I have included muffins in the dessert section, which usually are eaten as a snack or sometimes even as a meal. You can certainly eat them as a healthful alternative if you are weaning your family off traditional North American snacks such as pretzels, proteins bars, or cheese and crackers because the serving size is very small. If you look at the ingredient list of common pre-packaged snacks, you will find ingredients such as white flour, salt, sugar, high fructose corn syrup, and hydrogenated oils that have been heated at high temperatures. My muffins are more wholesome but they do contain coconut crystals, so I list them as a dessert. It is best to consider them as such and eat them in moderation.

You will be doing some baking in this section. I typically do not preheat my oven because it is a more environmentally conscious choice as this practice uses less energy. My recipes are written in this way and the baking times designated account for this practice.

Strawberry Chiffon Pie

Makes 8 servings

Hidden Treasures: rhubarb, sunchokes, and cauliflower

This dish is rich and creamy and makes for a wonderful side to a bowl of fruit for a light yet filling breakfast meal. It is best eaten when fresh local organic strawberries and rhubarb are available.

2 ½ cups strawberries, cut in half with stems left on
1 sweet apple
½ cup ripe mashed banana
½ cup rhubarb, chopped
1 sunchoke, chopped
¼ cup psyllium or arrowroot (thickening agent, so use more if needed)
1 strawberry and mint leaves for garnish (optional)

Put the strawberries, apple, banana, rhubarb, sunchoke, and psyllium in a high-powered blender. Pour the filling into the crust and refrigerate until the mixture becomes thick, at least 1 hour. Garnish with sliced strawberries and mint leaves.

Banana Soft Serve

Makes 4 servings

Hidden Treasure: cashew butter

This dessert is so healthful that I hesitate to include it in the dessert section. It just proves that desserts can in fact be good for you and can double as real meals. You can serve this up for breakfast with a buffet of add-ons such as berries, oats, hemp seeds, dates, sunflower seeds, and almonds, or you can enjoy as a traditional dessert with Hazelnut-Chocolate Spread (page 113).

4 ripe bananas
¼ cup cashew butter (optional)
1 teaspoon vanilla extract

Freeze chunks of ripe banana. Put the bananas, cashew butter, and vanilla into a food processor and pulse for 1–2 minutes until the mixture resembles soft serve. Serve immediately.

Hazelnut-Chocolate Spread

Makes 6 servings

Hidden Treasures: almonds, avocado, hazelnuts, and dates

The kids who eat Nutella on white bread for lunch inspired this recipe. Instead of spreading Nutella, consider this version as it is packed full of nutrients. It is in the dessert section because it tastes rich and creamy, but it could be served on whole sprouted grain bread as a meal or with fruit as a snack. I particularly enjoy mixing it with Fruit Dip (page 52) and layering it on cupcakes.

1 cup Nut Milk (page 33) or unsweetened store-bought option
1 small avocado, ripe
½ cup hazelnuts
½ cup raw cacao powder
12 large pitted dates

Put the milk, avocado, nuts, cacao, and dates in a blender. Turn blender on low, gradually working up to a full speed. Process until smooth, stopping to scrape the sides of the blender as needed while moving the mixture towards the blades. Stored in a glass jar in the refrigerator, the spread will last 1 week.

Tasty Gem: Cacao is the indigenous word for cocoa. If you cannot find raw cacao at your local store, shop online instead (see Suppliers for suggested retailers).

Variation: Substitute carob powder for the cacao powder if you are trying to avoid the stimulant Theobromine and add ½ teaspoon of vanilla extract.

Banana Bread Muffins

Makes 12 servings

Hidden Treasures: chia seeds, walnuts, and spinach

This banana bread is made with whole wheat flour and sweetened with bananas and maple syrup. They taste fabulous all on their own or you can top them with creamy cashew butter.

2 tablespoons chia seeds
6 tablespoons water
1 ½ cups whole wheat flour
1 ½ teaspoons baking powder
½ teaspoon ground cinnamon
½ cup Nut Milk (see page 33) or store-bought option
¼ cup coconut oil
½ teaspoon vanilla extract
1 cup maple syrup
2 cups mashed bananas (about 3 ripe bananas)
½ cup ground walnuts
½ cup shredded spinach

Put the seeds and water into a small bowl. Allow the mixture to sit until a gel is formed, stirring every couple of minutes.

Stir together the flour, baking powder, and cinnamon in a medium bowl. In a large bowl, mix the nut milk, coconut oil, vanilla extract, maple syrup, and bananas using a high-speed mixer. With the mixture running on low, slowly add in the flour mixture. Add the walnuts and spinach and blend until they are disguised.

Pour the batter into a muffin tin lightly coated with coconut oil. Bake for 1 hour at 250 degree F. Let cool and serve.

Pumpkin Bites

Makes 12 servings

Hidden Treasures: flax seeds, pumpkin, squash, and carrots

These bites are wonderfully delicious and are easy to take on the go. Pop several of them in your mouth for a quick fix and enjoy how the soft interior is luxuriously wrapped in a hard crust.

2 tablespoons ground flax seeds
6 tablespoons water
¼ cup carrot, chopped
¼ cup yellow squash
1 cup maple syrup
½ cup coconut oil
2 ¼ cups whole wheat flour
1 tablespoon pumpkin pie spice
½ teaspoon baking soda
1 ¼ cups cooked pumpkin
6 large pitted dates, chopped (optional)

Put the seeds and water in a small bowl until a gel forms, stirring occasionally.

Finely chop the carrots and squash in a food processor. Transfer the mixture to an electric standing mixer. Add the gel, syrup, and oil. Blend well.

Put the flour, pumpkin pie spice, and baking soda in a medium bowl and mix with a wooden spoon. Slowly add the flour mixture into the chia mixture while the machine is on a low speed until a wet batter is formed. Add the pumpkin meat and blend. Stir in the dates and pour the batter evenly into a muffin tin lightly coated with coconut oil. Put the pan in the oven and bake the bread for 40 minutes at 250 degrees F.

Gina D. Diamond, M.Ed.

Cranberry-Orange Muffins

Makes 12 servings

Hidden Treasures: chia seeds, pecans, and beets

This is a nice variation of the traditional cranberry pumpkin combination, especially if you like a slightly sweeter flavor. You may make these with or without cranberries depending on whether your family likes lumps in their muffins. I prefer to use the berries because they taste yummy and act as a great camouflage.

1 tablespoon chia seeds
3 tablespoons water
1 cup whole spelt flour
1 cup freshly squeezed orange juice
½ cup maple syrup (preferably grade B)
1 teaspoon baking soda
¼ cup ground pecans
1 teaspoon vanilla extract
½ cup finely shredded red beet (half of a small beet)
½–1 cup store-bought dried cranberries, preferably sweetened with apple juice

Put the seeds and water into a small bowl until a gel forms, stirring occasionally.

Stir the flour, orange juice, maple syrup, and baking soda in a medium bowl. Make a well in the center of the flour mixture and add the chia gel, pecans, vanilla, beets, and cranberries. Mix by hand until all the ingredients are well blended. Pour the mixture evenly into a lightly oiled muffin tin. Cook for 40 minutes at 250 degree F.

Nutritional Nugget: Chia seeds are a superfood that are known to increase energy and are packed with omega oils, protein, antioxidants, and fiber.

Wild Rice Muffins

Makes 12 servings

Hidden Treasures: wild rice, chia seeds, almonds, and zucchini

If your child balks at the sight of wild rice let him or her get their fill by eating these wonderful muffins. The chia seeds and zucchini add a nice nutrient punch while the rice adds a slightly nutty taste.

1 tablespoon chia seeds
3 tablespoons water
1 ½ cups whole spelt flour
¾ cup coconut crystals or maple syrup
1 teaspoon baking soda
¼ cup fruit-sweetened millet rice cereal
¾ cup cooked wild rice
½ cup coconut oil
½ cup Nut Milk (page 33) or unsweetened store-bought option
1 teaspoon vanilla extract
½ cup shredded zucchini

Put the seeds and water into a small bowl until a gel forms, stirring occasionally.

Stir the flour, crystals, baking soda, and cereal in a medium bowl. Set aside. Using an electric stand mixer combine the rice, coconut oil, milk, vanilla, and chia gel. Slowly add the flour mixture to the rice mixture and process until creamy. Add the zucchini and blend.

Spoon the batter evenly into a muffin tin that has been coated with coconut oil. Cook for 40 minutes at 250 degree F.

Gina D. Diamond, M.Ed.

Date-Banana Balls

Makes 25 servings

Hidden Treasures: quinoa and seeds

Packed full of powerful nutrient-rich ingredients, these dessert balls are sure to please. The mixture is also great eaten as cereal. Top with "Plant a Seed" Milk (page 34) or Nut Milk (page 33) and enjoy.

12 large pitted dates, chopped
2 tablespoons ground flaxseeds
6 tablespoons water
4 ripe bananas, chopped
1 teaspoon hemp seeds (optional)
1 cup cooked quinoa
1 cup oats
Cinnamon, to coat (optional)

Soak the dates in water for 5 minutes to soften. Combine the flaxseeds and the water into a small bowl until a gel forms, stirring occasionally.

Blend the bananas, hemp seeds, quinoa, and soaked dates in a medium bowl. Add the oats and flax gel and mix again. Form the mixture into small balls and lightly sprinkle them with cinnamon. Place them on a baking sheet that has been lightly coated with coconut oil.

Bake for 30 minutes at 250 degrees F, flipping half-way through. The date-banana balls with last 1 month in an airtight container.

Nutritional Nugget: Flaxseeds are difficult to soak at home so it is best to purchase an organic pre-sprouted variety produced by a reputable company if possible.

Pear-Plum Layered Cake

Makes 12 servings

Hidden Treasures: cauliflower and walnuts

This cake requires a bit more preparation than other desserts but it is worth the effort. The layered effect of the crust and fruit makes for a doughy yet sweet and creamy texture.

4 tablespoons ground flaxseeds
12 tablespoons water
3 cups whole wheat flour
1 ½ teaspoons baking powder
1 tablespoon ground cinnamon, divided
2 cups maple syrup or coconut nectar, divided
5 ripe pears, peeled and cut into cubes, divided
1 cup coconut butter
1 cup diced cauliflower
⅓ cup freshly squeezed orange juice
2 teaspoons vanilla extract
3 tablespoons ground walnuts
3 ripe plums, sliced

Put the seeds and water into a small bowl until a gel forms, stirring occasionally.

Combine the flour, baking powder, and half of the cinnamon in a medium bowl. Gently hand stir a third of the sweetener with the remaining cinnamon and half the pears. Set aside.

Beat the butter and cauliflower in an electric standing mixer until crumbly. Add the remaining sweetener and flax mixture and blend well. Slowly mix in the flour mixture. Add the orange juice, vanilla, and walnuts, blending until smooth.

Spoon ⅓ of the batter into a 9 x 2 inch round cake pan lightly coated with coconut oil. Spread out the batter evenly and then top with the remaining pear mixture, followed by a second layer of batter and a second layer of pears. Scoop the last remaining batter as a top coat and place sliced plums in a decorative pattern as a finishing touch.

Bake the cake for 1 hour and 15 minutes at 350 degrees F.

Gina D. Diamond, M.Ed.

Blackberry-Apple Crumble

Makes 8 servings

Hidden Treasures: beets, red pepper, and coconut oil

This recipe is fun to make during blackberry picking session and can be eaten raw by replacing the wheat flour with any type of nut flour. The blackberries are lightly sweetened by the apple and hide the vegetables very well.

Topping:
1 cup whole wheat flour
¼ cup coconut nectar or maple syrup
¼ cup coconut oil

Filling:
1 cup sweet apple, cubed
¼ cup shredded red beets
¼ cup shredded red peppers
3 cups fresh blackberries
1 tablespoon maple syrup (optional)

To make the topping, combine the flour, nectar, and oil using an electric standing mixer until a crumbly consistency is formed. Set aside.

Mix the apple pieces, beets, peppers, and blackberries in a 9 x 1 ¼ inch pie pan. Taste and add sweetener if desired. Sprinkle the crumble over the fruit mixture and bake for 45 minutes at 350 degrees F. Serve warm.

Variation: Add an additional ¼ cup of flour and replace the coconut nectar with coconut crystals if you want more of a crumble feel to the crust.

Nutritional Nugget: Psyllium and arrowroot powders are both natural thickeners. Psyllium is derived from gel-coated seeds while arrowroot is a tuber. Both are touted as having a positive health impact on the body.

Ginger Cookies

Makes 25 cookies

Hidden Treasures: molasses, almonds, ginger, and eggplant

These cookies are so tasty, kids have been known to eat the raw dough right out of the mixing bowl. The recipe is simple yet full of healthful ingredients. Enjoy!

⅓ cup solid coconut oil
½ cup maple syrup
¼ cup molasses
¼ cup Nut Milk (page 33) or unsweetened store-bought option
2 ¼ cups whole spelt flour
1 teaspoon baking soda
½ teaspoon ground cinnamon
1 teaspoon pumpkin pie spice
1 ½ teaspoons dried minced ginger
½ cup grated eggplant

Blend the oil, syrup, molasses, and milk in the bowl of an electric standing mixer. Set aside.

Mix the flour, baking soda, cinnamon, pie spice, and ginger in a medium bowl. Slowly pour the flour mixture into the oil mixture while blending on low. Add the eggplant and continue mixing for 30 seconds. Cut the dough into small mounds and lay them on cookie sheets that have lightly coated with coconut oil. Bake for 8–10 minutes at 350 degrees F.

Tasty Gems: Try substituting fresh shredded ginger for dried at a ratio of 6 to1.
Also, any kind of eggplant will do but silver eggplants work really well in this recipe.

Chocolate Brownie Cake

Makes 12 servings

Hidden Treasures: walnuts, beets, mint leaves, and almonds

This brownie cake is a tad less sweet than the kind you can purchase from a store but kids adore it anyway. It is moist and has the perfect balance between sweet and savory. Eat them like brownies or turn them into a chocolate cake smothered in Fruit Dip (page 52) or Chocolate Hazelnut Spread (page 113).

2 tablespoons ground flaxseeds
6 tablespoons water
¼ cup whole walnuts
⅛ cup chopped red beet
5 mint leaves
1 cup maple syrup (preferably grade B)
½ cup baking cocoa
1 cup whole wheat flour
1 teaspoon baking soda
1 teaspoon vanilla extract
1 ½ cups Nut Milk (page 33) or unsweetened store-bought option

Put the seeds and water into a small bowl until a gel forms, stirring occasionally.

Put the walnuts, beets, and mint leaves in a food processor. Grind until well blended and set aside. Combine the maple syrup, cocoa, flour, and baking soda in a medium bowl. Blend the vanilla, milk, and flax gel in an electric stand mixing bowl. Pour the flour mixture into the liquid mixture while blending continuously. Add the walnut mixture and continue to blend. Pour the cake mixture into a 9-inch square pan that has been lightly coated with coconut oil. Bake for 1 hour and 15 minutes at 250 degrees F.

Variation: Replace ½ cup cocoa with ½ cup raw carob powder.

Strawberry Almond Freeze

Makes 4 servings

Hidden Treasures: Strawberry hulls, almonds, kale, and seeds

This amazing treat contains fruit sugar so it is great for those who are limiting refined sugar in their diet. Enjoy alone or use it to top Wholesome Pancakes (page 25) for a sweet refreshing start to your morning.

10 strawberries, sliced with hulls intact
½ cup Nut Milk (page 33) or unsweetened store-bought option
10 small pitted dates, sliced
1 large kale leaf, torn
1 tablespoon sesame seeds

Put the strawberries, milk, dates, kale, and seeds into a high-speed blender. Begin mixing on a low speed, gradually working up to the highest speed until the mixture is smooth. Pour the mixture into a large empty yogurt container and place in the freezer. Freeze solid and let the sorbet defrost for several minutes before serving.

Nutritional Nugget: Strawberry hulls give a slight nutrient boost to this dessert as they contain minerals and chloropyll.

Minty Chip Ice

Makes 4 servings

Hidden Treasures: mint, tahini, and spiralina

This sorbet is as good as any store-bought option but with a lot more nutritional value. The mint is refreshing and is a great disguise for the spiralina powder. Use the recipe as a base for any flavor allowing your creative juices to flow.

2 cups Coconut Magic Milk (page 35) or store-bought, dairy-free milk
2 cups Date Water (page 40)
½ cup loosely packed mint leaves
4 tablespoons maple syrup
2 tablespoons tahini
10 large pitted dates, soaked
1 teaspoon spiralina powder (optional)
¼ cup cacao nibs

Put the coconut milk, date water, mint leaves, crystals, tahini, dates, and spiralina in a high-speed blender. Blend on high until the texture is smooth. Pour the liquid into a reusable ice cream container and stir in the cacao nibs. Put in the freezer until frozen solid and eat when ready.

Nutritional Nugget: Spiralina is a micro-algae that contains large amounts of chlorophyll, is a heavy metal detoxifier, and contains a large amount of protein.

Variation: Replace 4 tablespoons of maple syrup with 1 large banana for a creamy texture and replace ¼ cup of cacao nibs with ¼ cup fairly traded chocolate chips for a sweeter taste.

Strawberry Cream Frosting

Makes 4 servings

Hidden Treasures: cashews and beets

This raw frosting is a great topping to just about any type of dessert. Enjoy with ice cream, Brownies (page 122), or organic fresh fruit, but beware as it tastes great all by itself and it might not make it past the mixing bowl before it is totally consumed.

2 cups raw cashews
½ cup coconut nectar or maple syrup
4 strawberries, sliced with hulls intact
1 medium red beet, chopped
2 tablespoons coconut butter
½ teaspoon vanilla extract

Soak the cashews in water for 8 hours. Drain and rinse the nuts. Put them in a blender with the nectar, strawberries, beets, coconut butter, and vanilla. Blend well. Pour the frosting into a repurposed plastic bag and cut off one of the tips. Squeeze the frosting out of the bag and onto your dessert. Set in the refrigerator to thicken the mixture as necessary. The frosting will keep for 1–2 weeks in a glass container in the refrigerator.

Nutritional Nugget: Coconut butter is a whole food made of pure, dried coconut flesh. It is different than coconut oil.

Conclusion:

The hidden treasures method has worked really well for my family. I certainly have gotten my daughter and her friends to eat a lot more nutrient-dense foods since implementing this simple idea. As my daughter grew older, I began explaining the concept. She now knows that I put hidden treasures into pretty much anything that can easily be used as a disguise and it helps that she is a lot less picky. The trick is to get family members to try things first before telling them what is on the ingredient list. They tend to be more open and receptive to cauliflower in their granola if they discover how delicious it tastes before I tell them my surprise. The main reason I eventually divulge my ingredient lists is because I want them to understand the importance of eating well so that they can have this information when they are out in the world making their own choices. I also want children to think that this is a normal way to prepare food, encouraging them to carry it forward in their own lives. You will be amazed at how cutting out highly processed meals and snacks that contain refined sugars, salts, and oils and replacing them with healing foods will change their taste buds and physical composition. Do not be surprised if you family members begin to reject pretzels and ask for kale chips instead.

Nutritional Nugget: The Grand Prix: Now that you have tried several recipes, it is time to congratulate yourself. Incorporating positive habits to create a new lifestyle takes time, energy, and courage. You are a brave parent and your family is lucky to have you. Take a moment, or preferably a day, to do something nice for yourself as a way to celebrate and renew your commitment to healthful living. Perhaps you can treat yourself to an organic day spa or spend a few hours in nature by yourself. It is amazing how a little self-care can help you stay motivated and on target with your ultimate goal. Keep going and please connect to our online community for additional ideas and support.

Glossary

Amaranth: Amaranth is a seed that is referred to as a pseudograin. It is a protein powerhouse and good for your heart. It is the only "grain" that contains vitamin C, and it is gluten-free, as well.

Arrowroot starch: Arrowroot starch is a natural thickener made from the arrowroot plant. Dissolve arrowroot in a small amount of cool liquid before adding to sauces, gravies, pie fillings, or puddings. After adding, bring to a boil, stirring constantly, then lower the heat and cook until thickened.

Bok choy: Bok choy is a leafy Chinese cabbage that is full of fiber and vitamins, such as A, B, C, K and minerals, calcium and iron.

Brazil nuts: Brazil nuts are very high in selenium and host many other vitamins and minerals including vitamins B and E, copper, magnesium, calcium, and iron.

Buckwheat groats: Buckwheat groats are high in iron, protein, fiber, vitamins, alpha lipoic acid, and essential fatty acid. You get a lot of bang for your buck with these nuggets, and many kids will eat them because they have a nutty flavor.

Cherimoya: Cherimoya is a tropical fruit that tastes sweet and is high in vitamins B and C, potassium, and antioxidants.

Chia Seeds: Chia seeds are a superfood that date back to the Aztecs. They are known to increase energy and are packed with omega-3, protein, antioxidants, and fiber.

Chlorella: Chlorella is a micro-algae that contains large amounts of chlorophyll, which reduces inflammation and renews blood and body tissues.

Coconut Butter: Coconut butter refers to the whole meat of a coconut. You may see this labeled as coconut manna.

Coconut palm sugar (crystals and nectar): Coconut palm sugar is the sweet water sap derived from cut coconut flower buds. Distinct in taste but wonderfully good nevertheless, coconut sugar is a great sweetener because it is a whole food and contains vitamins and minerals.

Coconut oil. Coconut oil is the oil extracted from coconut meat.

Cold pressed: Cold pressed is a chemical-free mechanical process that extracts oil from seeds and nuts. The United States government does not regulate this term or the temperature at which cold pressing is legally defined, so be sure to pick your brand carefully.

EFA oil: Oil that is derived from products that contain essential fatty acids. Look for a pure, unrefined, organic, and cold-pressed variety.

Extra-virgin: Extra-virgin refers to oil that comes from the first pressing (see cold pressed above).

Fair Trade: Fair Trade is a certification that aims to guarantee that exports from developing countries to developed countries are produced by high social and environmental standards such as equitable pay and healthy working conditions.

Farro: Farro is a wheat grain in whole form. It can be ground into flour, eaten as cereal, or used in place of rice. Be sure to soak this grain before consuming.

Heirloom: Heirloom refers to a type of produce that is grown from seeds handed down from generation to generation as compared to modern hybrids. Heirlooms produce food that is more nutritious and often tastes better.

Hemp seeds: Hemp seeds are known as a superfood because of its high nutrient count and because it is a durable crop that offers high yields. It is currently illegal to grow hemp plants in the United States.

Kabocha: Kabocha is a type of winter squash that is very popular among adults and kids alike. Its flavor resembles a sweet potato when cooked and it can be used in many recipes or eaten by itself.

Kelp powder. Kelp powder is a sea vegetable that has been ground into a powder.

Maca: Maca is a root often sold in powder form that is believed to help the body deal with stress while increasing energy and endurance.

Miner's lettuce: Miner's lettuce is a succulent herb grown as a pot herb and can be found in the wild. It has an extremely mild taste and is lovely eaten raw as a side, in salads, and smoothies.

Miso: Miso is a salty, flavorful, fermented paste that often contains soy, rice, barley, or another grain or legume. Because it is fermented it has probiotic properties and adds a nice seasoning to soups, salad dressings, and spreads.

Moringa *Oleifera*: The most nutrient-dense plant discovered on Earth. To get it in its best form contact me at gina@consciouslivingstrategist.com.

Nettles: Nettles are an herb that can be foraged or grown at home. Look for dried varieties at your health food store.

Nori: Nori is a sea vegetable that is incredibly nutrient dense. It is usually found in the ethnic aisle at grocery stores. It comes in black (roasted) or green (unroasted).

Nutritional yeast: Nutritional yeast is an inactive yeast that has a nutty, cheesy flavor and is a favorite among vegetarians as it contains B-12, a vitamin that is hard to find in plant foods. It is sometimes referred to as nooch.

Oat groats: Oat groats are the kernel that rolled oats are derived from. They are a less processed product. They can be ground into flour, used in place of rice, or eaten as cereal.

Probiotics: Probiotics are found in fermented food such as miso, tempeh, sauerkraut and kefir. They promote healthful digestion by maintaining the natural balance of microflora in the intestines.

Pseudograins: Pseudograins are a product that comes from a plant that resembles a grain but is really a seed, such quinoa and amaranth.

Quinoa: Quinoa is a seed that is referred to as a pseudograin. This product does not contain gluten, cooks much quicker than rice, and is very versatile.

Spirulina: Spirulina is a blue-green micro-algae that is consumed as a whole food or in a supplement. It is available in tablet, flake, or powder form.

Sulfite: Sulfite is an additive chemical used to preserve foods and is a common food allergen. Prepackaged dried fruit are often sulfured. Sulfites are also found in nature.

Sunchoke: Sunchokes are a root vegetable that is often referred to as a Jerusalem artichoke. They can be eaten raw or cooked.

Raw: The definition of raw varies depending on what "expert" you talk to. I typically consider my food raw if it is cooked (usually dehydrated) at a temperature below 115 degrees F.

Tahini: Tahini is a creamy paste made from finely ground raw or roasted sesame seeds. It has a nutty flavor and is most commonly used in Middle Eastern recipes such as hummus and babaganoush. It is best to store tahini in the refrigerator to keep it from becoming rancid and to keep the oil from separating out. If the oil does separate out, simply stir it back in. Raw tahini is easier to find online than in stores.

Suppliers

Azure Standards

https://bit.ly/2MgaGHn

This is an online bulk delivery food company that specializes in natural and organic food. They even own their own farm and sell their own produce. A minimum order is required, so going in with neighbors is helpful. You will save money buy choosing Azure.

Bright Earth Foods

www.brightearthfoods.com
Bright Earth is a superfood company that a friend of mine owns. He is extremely dedicated to sourcing the best food grown on the planet.

Conscious Living Strategist Blog

http://consciouslivingstrategist.tumblr.com/
This is the companion blog to this book where you will find all things delicious. You will be able to purchase some of the things called for in this book. You can also connect with families who are implementing the hidden treasures method, receive tips to staying motivated, and get additional recipes and bigger ideas of how to live more deliciously.

Garden of Life

www.gardenoflife.com
Garden of Life sells raw, organic, whole food supplements in the form of tablets and powders. They claim to source their ingredients from farmers who go beyond organics. Their products contain vegetables, superfoods, and unique product that are difficult to

find in regular grocery stores. They sell a whole food supplement for children, which is low in fruit sugar.

Hidden Treasures

www.HiddenTreasureRecipes.com
Here you will find the companion website to this book.

About the Author

As the Nutrition Strategist™, Gina Diamond is dedicated to helping people live a more delicious life. By sharing easy-to-implement solutions, she helps her clients feel better, have more energy, and begin to love their bodies. Her work is centered on supporting women and the people they influence, so that they and their families experience improved mental, physical, and spiritual health.

Although Diamond loves real food and strives to find simple ways to prepare meals that promote well-being, she once struggled with her own health. After developing numerous conditions, including depression and anxiety, she discovered that her body could heal if she gave it what it needed to function properly. After Diamond had a child and witnessed a typical public school lunch, she became motivated to help by creating mealtime solutions that even the most exhausted parents and teachers could implement.

Diamond wrote *Hidden Treasures* with her own picky eater in mind. This book offers achievable solutions for those who want to do right by their kids nutritionally. Inspired by *Cooking for the Whole Family* by Cynthia Lair and with her main solution confirmed by the best aspects of Jessica Seinfeld's *Deceptively Delicious*, Diamond knew it was time to share what had worked so well for her family and her wellness coaching clients, which include hundreds of parents, the Port of Seattle, Google, CoolMoms, and One Sky Wellness.

To learn more about nourishing your body, mind, and soul, visit consciousnutritionstrategies.com.

Printed in the United States
By Bookmasters